Charles & Diana

INSIDE A ROYAL MARRIAGE

JUDY WADE

Eden

Acknowledgements
The author would like to thank Arthur Edwards and
Harry Arnold, the leaders of the pack, for
their unfailing support and encouragement
and is also grateful for the help
of dozens of friends at Court.

Cover picture and all inside photographs
by Arthur Edwards

EDEN PAPERBACKS
an imprint of Angus & Robertson Publishers

Unit 4, Eden Park, 31 Waterloo Road,
North Ryde, NSW, Australia 2113, and
16 Golden Square, London W1R 4BN,
United Kingdom

First published in the United Kingdom
by Angus & Robertson (UK) in 1987
First published in Australia
by Angus & Robertson Publishers in 1987

Copyright © Judy Wade 1987

British Library Cataloguing in Publication Data
Wade, Judy
    Charles and Diana: inside a royal marriage.
    1. Charles: Prince of Wales – Marriage
    2. Diana: Princess of Wales – Marriage
    i. Title
    941.085'092'2   DA 591.A33
    ISBN 0-207-15688-3
Typeset by New Faces, Bedford
Printed in Great Britain by
Richard Clay Ltd, Bungay, Suffolk

Contents

1

Separate Lives?

'When we first got married we were everyone's idea of the world's most perfect, ideal couple. Now they say we're leading separate lives. The next thing I know I'll read in some newspaper that I've got a black lover.'

Princess Diana was chatting to a group of journalists at a cocktail party in Madrid when a photographer, bolder than the rest of us, posed the question that was on all our minds in the spring of 1987. What was the truth behind the stories that Charles and Diana, the world's most famous lovers, were drifting apart?

Her answer tumbled out totally straight. The very idea that she was ever half of a perfect couple was clearly as ridiculous as her imaginary lover. Forget it! A passing waiter offered a tray of drinks. And as she sipped a glass of iced mineral water the Princess cheerfully predicted that no matter what she said, someone somewhere would surely reveal soon that she had a secret lover. It was only a matter of time before the banner headlines were out on the streets.

Could this perky Princess be the dejected girl regularly dumped at home, according to all the rumours, by her eccentric old man?

'The truth about our separate lives is very simple,' she insisted. 'My husband and I get around 2,000 invitations to visit different places every six months. We couldn't possibly get through many if we did them all together. So we have

1

decided to accept as many as we can separately. This means we can get to twice as many places and see twice as many people.'

Her face was winter pale with barely a trace of make-up. But as every woman in the room noted enviously, she looked a knockout nonetheless in a slinky black skirt and swish silk taffeta top. A little designer number worn with drop-dead flair, its stiff, standout sleeves and padded shoulders exaggerated every snaky shrug.

Her hair was definitely longer, her heels much higher. Gliding around groups of Spanish and British journalists gathered to meet her at the El Pardo palace, the Princess of Wales was obviously enjoying herself. No probing question could cause the slightest flicker in those confident blue eyes.

Her once scrawny figure also seemed more rounded. She laughed a lot, she teased one reporter about his flash tie and she ticked off another. His crime was a centrespread claiming that the royal couple were reversing their roles at home. 'I've got a bone to pick with you,' she said stalking over to him, then declared his story was total nonsense.

Prince Charles was planning another of his solo trips, she later confided to us, apparently unruffled by the thought that this might set the gossips off again. She beamed like any proud wife as she explained that: 'It's something my husband has wanted to do all his life.'

Diana still did not look at all dismayed when exactly one week later at the end of a tour of Spain Prince Charles kissed his wife goodbye. As she headed home to see their sons William and Harry, he flew off to Bologna in Italy to collect an award for sales of his children's storybook *The Old Man of Lochna'gar*. Afterwards he stayed on in Padua and Florence to visit old friends and sketch the Tuscan hills.

It was his third trip to Italy without his wife in little more than a year. And in the first six months of 1987 he had deserted her on four other occasions. In February he had stayed on in Switzerland skiing after his wife flew back home to work. In March he returned to the Alps alone spending a long weekend in Gstaad with friends. Then early in April after a tour of southern Africa he had disappeared into the Kalahari desert with author and mystic Sir Laurens van der Post. And a month later he left his family again to spend three days salmon fishing in the River Dee. It seemed a strange way to stay married. Separate jobs were understandable but separate holidays quite another matter.

Suddenly Diana's little joke about finding a lover did not seem so funny. And she had got it slightly wrong. Within days the world was wondering if he, not she, had strayed.

While he was in Italy Prince Charles' name was tenuously linked with that of a beautiful Contessa whom he had met several times before on visits to Italy. Despite furious denials from the family of Fiammetta Frescobaldi, heiress to one of Italy's greatest fortunes, rumours about Charles' Italian Job persisted.

As usual, Buckingham Palace did not condescend to issue any hot denials. Perhaps there was nothing to deny. But the Prince's press officer had also failed to give advance notice of Charles' trip to Italy, the first time anyone could remember this happening. In fact, the award ceremony in Bologna had been announced in Italy some months earlier but not in London. It was missing from his list of engagements for April 1987.

Didn't the Prince want the world to know about the award and where he was going? And if so, why? Fleet Street's royal correspondents thought all this was rather odd. Had there been an attempt at a cover-up? In which case was it the Contessa or his fourth holiday in four months that Prince Charles hoped we wouldn't find out about? Before his marriage the Prince had surrounded himself with sophisticated, intelligent beauties, mostly blonde and many of them married. He had been very close to Dale, Lady Tryon, a glamorous Australian he fondly called 'Kanga'. He had also remained on the friendliest terms with Camilla Parker-Bowles, a girl once tipped as a possible bride for the Prince until she married a cavalry officer with the Blues and Royals. Reporters recalled that he has always enjoyed the stimulating company of women who share his passion for the arts. It wasn't surprising if he selected one or two as guides to the glories of the Italian Renaissance. Or was it?

His return to Tuscany inevitably set people wondering why Charles and Diana seemed to go their separate ways so often. It seemed a startling contrast to the early days of their marriage. When the Prince had left his bride just two months after their wedding to attend the funeral of Egypt's assassinated President Sadat, Diana had cried bitterly when left behind. For a year or two afterwards they had astonished and delighted onlookers by smooching openly in public. At airports, on the dance floor, behind horse boxes and even in front of spectators at the Braemar Highland Games their clinches kept on coming. They sometimes had rows right in front of everyone too. But anyone could see Charles was daft about Diana. Royal reserve was a thing of the past for the once stiff and starchy Prince.

As their sixth wedding anniversary approached things had changed. Now it seemed he deserted her at every opportunity. And she had to find her own fun going out on the town with a younger crowd. Had the world's most famous marriage lost its magic? For some time it had looked as if they were rapidly drifting in opposite directions.

The commentators who once got carried away describing how cleverly Diana had saved the Wales now decided it was all her fault. She was hardly a brilliant match mentally for a man educated to be a king, they noted. She had failed her O-levels not once but twice, he on the other hand, had left Cambridge with a second-class history degree. What could this couple possibly have in common?

Diana had always mixed with a group of SuperSloane friends who apparently had little interest in world affairs, her critics pointed out. Her husband had been influenced from birth by men of maturity and experience. Everyone knew that Charles looked on Sir Laurens van der Post as his own personal guru. While she loved to curl up with slushy novels or books about herself, her husband got stuck into heavy stuff about anthropology, architecture or reports on inner-city slums.

Then one well-connected woman repeated a hot item she had learned first hand. It came from a hostess who had recently entertained the royal couple at a weekend house party. Charles and Diana had insisted on separate bedrooms!

This news hardly galloped around the shires, where elderly dowagers could barely remember how long it had been since their husbands had moved into the dressing room. Didn't every upper-class couple have separate duvets?

But eventually, via the Sloane Zone of Fulham, Chelsea and South Kensington, the story drifted down to Fleet Street. Diana herself no doubt unwittingly fuelled the fires of gossip by telling an astonishing number of people that she had decided to take a long break from pregnancy after the birth of her second son. 'I'm not a production line, you know,' she said tartly at the end of 1985 when a woman who met her on a walkabout asked if a third baby was on the way.

No curious journalist dared ask such an impertinent question. But none needed to. 'By the way, I'm not at the moment,' the Princess declared with one hand significantly rubbing her stomach when she met the press on a tour of Portugal in February 1987.

Two months later in Spain she said it again. 'I'm too busy to have any babies for at least a year,' she said. 'I have to go to Australia next January.' Then she added mysteriously: 'You see, I'm safe,' again gesturing towards her stomach. Clearly the Princess was taking precautions that would guarantee no more babies for some time.

Charles has made no secret of the fact that he would like lots of children. But when he mentions this in public Diana makes a wry face at him. She does not find it easy to cope with the morning sickness and back aches that plague her during pregnancy. And his light-hearted comments often seem pointedly aimed at reminding his wife of her duty. Their opposing ideas on the size of their family look to many like growing evidence of a real rift between them.

But what lay behind that scandalous story about separate

bedrooms? 'It was so ridiculous I didn't even draw it to their attention,' said her exasperated press officer, Victor Chapman.

Fortunately, another royal aide even closer to the Princess decided to set the record straight. 'There is a very simple reason why they do have separate bedrooms when on tour or visiting friends,' he explained. 'When the Princess steps out of the shower in the morning she doesn't want her husband's valet in the room. For the same reason, the Prince doesn't want the Princess's maid there when he is putting on his underpants.

'Anyway, four people rushing around one bedroom – five if you count her hairdresser who calls later – would get in each other's way. The Prince and Princess are always in a great hurry to get up, get dressed and get out, so two bedrooms are much easier for everyone.'

When asked if the beds in each room were used the royal aide grinned and replied with exquisite delicacy. 'One would never ask such an intimate question, of course. But one can't help noticing that the Princess's clothes are laid out all over the place in her room. And they are still there next morning, which naturally leads one to the conclusion that only one bed is ever used.'

At weekend house parties their friends follow the upper-class custom of providing two separate rooms. That is the nearest they can come to making available something like the regal comforts Charles and Diana enjoy at home. At what they jokily call their Kensington council house the Prince and Princess share a luxurious suite of private rooms. The largest is a huge bedroom, the main feature of which is a king-size four poster bed stylishly swatched in blue fabric. Through a door on one side of the room Diana walks into her lavishly furnished dressing room and bathroom annexe.

One room is completely furnished with wardrobes packed with hundreds of outfits and matching accessories. The main dressing room is decorated in pale green and it is here that her hairstylist Richard Dalton prepares her for official engagements. The Prince has his own rather more modest dressing-room lined with closets and cupboards which hold his collection of more than 100 uniforms.

So much for the separate duvet rumour. But wasn't it still true that the royal couple rarely spent one night in the same house, let alone the same bed? For instance, when Charles and Diana flew to Balmoral in the spring of 1987 for a weekend break with their sons the Princess returned to London a day early. It was proof once again that Di could not endure another minute at boring Balmoral, or so the story went. She could not wait to ditch her husband and dash back to her own glitzy group of friends.The truth, however, her aide reported, was not so sensational. 'It was always planned that the Princess would leave Scotland before her husband and children. She had a day of appointments with her dress designers in London that simply could not be put off. To save money she had all the long dresses and skirts chosen for her 1986 tour of the Gulf States shortened to normal street length. But she had very little time for fittings before the start of her official visit to Spain where she wanted to wear them again.'

The Queen had invited the Wales family to Windsor for Easter the same week. There was no way, the aide explained, that the Princess could say to the Queen: 'Sorry, I have to leave the Easter court to meet my dressmakers in town.'

'It's infuriating that simple ordinary events in her life are totally misinterpreted by people who do not know the full facts,' he sighed. Prince Charles has also been depressed, but not really surprised, by the ever-wilder allegations about his marriage: 'They were saying the same things about my parents years ago,' he reminds friends. 'I think a new rumour started every time my father went off on *Britannia* somewhere.'

The one person who shrugs off these tall tales is the Princess of Wales. She still gets annoyed when she reads reports that her marriage is a misery, but she no longer bursts into tears, as she once did. 'I don't get the vapours any more, I think I am coping much better now,' she tells her friends.

The handful of people who see the Prince and Princess when they are out of the public gaze know a couple who care deeply about being together; people such as the ground staff at RAF Northolt, who saw the Princess waiting on the tarmac when her husband returned from his much-publicised trip to Italy, just as they have seen the Prince drive out to the airport late at night to meet his wife when she has been away on a job. They have noted the warm way they greet each other and drive off home with their arms around each other. The household at Highgrove smile, too, when they hear the boss call to his sons: 'Look, here comes the helicopter. Mummy's home. Let's go out and meet her.' Then two excited little boys rush out of the front door with their father, racing each other to be first to give Diana a welcome home kiss.

They also note that both the Prince and Princess try to keep Mondays clear of engagements so that they can be alone together at Highgrove, the place they call their retreat. They send their sons back to London on Sunday afternoons ready for school on Monday morning. Then Diana and Charles spend a cosy evening just relaxing together without interruption. Next morning they get up late, dawdle over breakfast and potter about the garden, then they return to duties in town as late as possible in the afternoon. Unless some very pressing duty intervenes they keep Mondays free just for each other.

In the privacy of their own home no one hears the Prince and Princess call each other anything but 'darling'. To the people who know them and their children best they seem like a very happy little family.

But if their lives are not as separate as they seem, their attitudes to their roles are changing. While her staff notice that the Princess tackles her job now with growing enthusiasm and self-assurance, her husband is a very different story.

2

A Search For Inner Peace

'You can't understand what it's like to have your whole life mapped out for you a year in advance. It's so awful to be programmed. I know what I'll be doing next week, next month, even next year. At times I get so fed up with the whole idea.'

Those few words, spoken as he stood chatting to journalists in February 1987, were probably the greatest clue that Charles, Prince of Wales, has ever let slip about his feelings towards his duty and his destiny.

He is a man set on a path through life that is not of his choosing – his privileged position is an accident of birth. If he had a choice, would he wish to be heir apparent to the only major monarch left on earth?

After following him around the world for several years I have my doubts. But Prince Charles has no choice. He has always known that it was his destiny to become not just a king but a servant of a system now obsolete in most countries of the world. He is being prepared to begin the world's most luxurious prison sentence.

He exists just to be gawked at and his private life is the subject of endless speculation. He can't think or say anything exceptional, if he does he is sure to upset someone. He has glory but no power. And instead of being able to look forward, as most people do, to a day when he can retire and do as he pleases, this man can never quit. Only death can release him from his responsibilities.

Charles is not the type to bolt the way his great uncle did. King Edward VIII, later Duke of Windsor, who was forced to live forever afterwards in exile, is also a hideous example of what happens to runaway kings.

But the Prince may often wish he could. He lives a life in limbo waiting for a job he dreads. How he must have envied his youngest brother Prince Edward when he dropped out of the Royal Marines. The Queen's youngest child proved he was man enough to join the most bone-crunching, back-breaking outfit in the armed forces. But when in January 1987 he decided halfway through training that the life was not for him he also had the guts to quit, as fourth in line of succession to the throne he had a freedom to opt out which his elder brother will always be denied.

'There are worse things than being born royal,' argues Harry Arnold, royal correspondent on the *Sun*. 'He could have been born physically or mentally handicapped.' It's true. Prince Charles is extremely privileged. A great position means great responsibilities. Noblesse must still oblige, and no one seems more conscious of this than the Prince.

But increasingly it looks as if Prince Charles wants to escape from his royal role. And, occasionally, he is so desperate to get away that any excuse is good enough to justify staying away from London and his official role.

On a mid-January morning in 1987 the royal estate of Sandringham was so thickly shrouded in snow that few roads were open. And those that had been cleared were blocked with slowly moving traffic. But the Prince of Wales, due back in London from Norfolk to attend the theatre that night, did not seem at all depressed by the weather. He borrowed a pair of cross-country skis from an equerry and set off down the drive of Sandringham House as cheerfully as if he were heading for the slopes at Klosters.

To a royal aide who looked surprised to find the Prince not dressed for the trip back to town Charles explained rather lamely: 'Well, I don't think I should add to the chaos on the roads, do you? I think I'll stay on here awhile.'

Not one member of the Royal Household dared to mention the fact that the Prince could easily have caught a train back to London from King's Lynn station eight miles away, as his cousin the Duke of Kent had done. That night the Princess of Wales went to the theatre in the West End of London alone.

The following morning was a big day in the life of Charles and Diana's elder son Prince William. It was his very first day as a full-time schoolboy. He was beginning his first term at Wetherby, an exclusive pre-prep school in Notting Hill, west London. The Buckingham Palace press office had previously announced that the Prince of Wales would go along to see this big step in his small son's life. But it was William's mother who held his hand as he stepped out of the family estate car and walked across the pavement to meet his new headmistress. The Prince had been unable to return to London for this important occasion because, claimed a palace spokesman, of the bad weather in Norfolk.

Charles frankly admits that he dislikes city life and is 'a countryman at heart', as he once put it. Returning to the capital, even for the sake of Prince William's first day at school, means going back to the less pleasant aspects of his life – mainly the business meetings and other desk work.

His intelligence and sensitivity also mean that when he goes out and about on official visits to rundown inner-city areas, he returns home questioning his own privileged lifestyle.

His big, brash brother Andrew has the kind of unquestioning attitude to his royal role which makes it easier to carry out. In fact, the Duke of York would be much preferred as a future king by some sections of the Establishment. Almost like a battery-operated robot he would no doubt go through the motions of being monarch without any sign of a troubled conscience.

The Queen has coped superbly with the job for thirty-five years. But unlike Charles she has never known any other life. She was poorly educated at home along very traditional lines, though she was exposed briefly to a simulation of the ordinary working world when she trained during the closing days of

11

World War II as a subaltern in the Auxiliary Territorial Service. At the age of eighteen she was chauffeur-driven each day to Aldershot in Surrey where, with a hand-picked team of the right sort of young women, she did a course on vehicle maintenance. Shortly after she finished training the war ended and so too did her glimpse of the real world.

She was married at a comparatively young age, had a family soon afterwards and became Queen at the age of twenty-five. Elizabeth never had time to dwell on whether she enjoyed her job, she was too busy getting on with it.

Charles, however, has led a totally different life. The best-prepared heir to the throne in history, he went to boarding school from the age of eight. He moved on to Gordonstoun School in Scotland and then spent seven months in Australia at Timbertop School in the bush outside Melbourne when he was seventeen. His equerry, Squadron Leader David Checketts, went with him taking his young family. Royal biographer Anthony Holden writing of this period recounts how Charles often joined them at their farmhouse at weekends. 'The Prince would muck in like a member of the family, coming down to breakfast in his dressing-gown, making his own bed, doing his share of the household chores.'

Looking back later on this period at Timbertop Charles said: 'I absolutely adored it. I couldn't have enjoyed it more. That school's probably the reason why, whenever I come back to Australia, I experience a curious and inexplicable sensation that I belong.'

Most of all he enjoyed the fact that the Aussies were not toadies impressed by his title. In fact, they were quite the reverse: there was no sucking up to him Down Under as there was at home. 'In Australia you are judged on how people see you and feel about you. There are no assumptions. You have to fend for yourself.'

After leaving Gordonstoun he won a place at Cambridge University with two A-levels, a Grade C in French and a B in history, with a distinction in the optional special paper which gave him an S-level. Only 6 per cent of other students gained such a distinction that year.

He joined Trinity College's drama club and enjoyed the humbling experience of having custard pies thrown in his face. He also played another scene sitting in a dustbin. He learned how to cook, do his own laundry, and got to know other students with political views radically different from his own. The first heir apparent ever to win a university degree, he left with a respectable second-class history BA.

But his real taste of freedom came when he joined the Royal Navy. In February 1976 he was given his own naval command, the mine-sweeper *HMS Bronnington*. When he left it at the end of that year he said: 'It's given me a marvellous opportunity to get as close to the "ordinary" British chap as possible.'

Long stretches at sea sharing the same cramped quarters as his fellow officers and without his Scotland Yard detective gave the Prince more independence than his mother could ever have dreamed of experiencing. But it had to be only a temporary taste of freedom. In 1977 Charles became a full-time royal waver and hand-shaker. After ten years marking time in his career, it would be understandable if he was beginning to get fed up with it.

The blessing and the curse of the Royal Family is that its women live to an advanced age. Now heading for her mid-sixties the Queen is so healthy and active she may easily reign for another twenty years or more. Her mother, although as old as the century, shows no signs of slowing up; the Queen's grandmother, Queen Mary, was eighty-six when she died in 1953, and the last woman who ruled in her own right, Queen Victoria, celebrated sixty years on the throne before she died at the age of eighty-two. Her son Bertie, then Prince of Wales, used to moan: 'I am cursed by an eternal mother.'

But Prince Charles certainly does not feel the same way. Far from being impatient to be king, he is apprehensive about taking over the top job in the family firm. Although repeated opinion polls show that the British people feel the Queen deserves to retire some day and enjoy a well-earned rest, neither she nor her son share this view. Charles once declared:

13

'I don't think monarchs should retire and be pensioned off, say at sixty, as some professions and businesses stipulate. The nature of being a monarch is different.

'Take Queen Victoria. In her eighties she was more loved, more known, more revered in her country than she'd ever been before. In other walks of life, too, age may bring accumulations of respect – and possibly wisdom – which are valuable to society.

'Looking at the monarchy as objectively as I can, I'd say retirement at a certain age is not a sensible idea. Some kind of unfitness is a different matter, but you must leave it to the monarch concerned. If you look outside this country, King Gustav of Sweden reigned until he was ninety. I think most people agree that Sweden would have lost something had he retired at sixty.'

The Prince's official spokesman, Victor Chapman, believes that he still holds the same views. 'If he were king he would not be able to do a lot of the things he does now. For a start, the Commonwealth countries would expect him to go around visiting their down-and-outs in their inner cities as well as Britain's. And then they would ask why the Princess didn't patronise their fashion designers instead of just ones in London. There would be a whole new range of restrictions on both their lives.'

When he is proclaimed King Charles III, the Prince will lose a lot that he holds dear now. He will have to move out of Highgrove House in Gloucestershire and leave his much-loved gardens there. His country home is much too small for a Head of State, and anyway the reigning monarch by tradition spends weekends at Windsor. There will be less time for polo in summer and hunting in winter – at present the Queen carries out almost twice as many royal engagements as Prince Charles.

Is it surprising, then, that the Prince hopes to avoid shouldering his mother's burden as long as he possibly can? Or that he tries to drop out briefly now, while he still can, and escape the soul-destroying tedium of life on the royal roundabout?

His wife also finds public appearances hard going, especially on tours abroad. After their first seven-week slog around Australia and New Zealand in 1983 Charles and Diana decided to undertake no more lengthy overseas trips. Most of their official visits to foreign countries now last little more than a week, or ten days at most.

'She absolutely loathes most tours,' claims a man on the Princess's staff. 'When she collapsed at Expo '86 in Canada some of us wondered if she was really exhausted or whether she was simply fed up with being dragged around one boring hall of exhibits after another. It seemed an incredible coincidence to us that at the precise moment she swooned there were no cameras in the room. Only one TV camera crew caught a very blurred, long distance shot of the incident. Very convenient, that was.'

After her initial excitement about seeing glamorous cities on the other side of the world, Diana began to look on touring as sheer hard work. She misses her children and is never happy until she is home with them again.

But while she likes nothing better than to romp around the nursery with her boys Prince Charles rarely has time to put his feet up at home. There is always a mountain of paperwork waiting for him in London or in the country. 'You should see the bags of official papers that follow him around wherever he goes,' explains a royal equerry. To get a total break from the drudgery of his duties Charles has to get right away into the desert, disappear up an Alp or take off for the Tuscan hills.

His only other outlet is physical exercise. And his favourite way to unwind has always been polo. The sport seems more of an obsession than a game to the Prince. He often says it saves his sanity. 'If I didn't get the exercise – or have something to take my mind off things – I would go potty.'

From the age of four Charles spent most summer weekends hanging around the edge of a polo field. Prince Philip, one of the high-goal players of his day, always found the game was a great release from the pressures of his royal role. 'One could almost see the steam coming out of him on a Saturday after the frustrations of a week of public engagements,' said Major Ronald Ferguson, then polo manager to the Queen's husband and now holding the same position with Prince Charles.

Anyone who has ever seen the Prince of Wales galloping flat out across Smith's Lawn polo ground, hanging half out of the saddle as he whacks another ball through the goal posts will understand that it does the same for him.

'I feel a hundred times better after a game of polo,' Charles once revealed. If he doesn't manage to get in some regular vigorous exercise, he admits that he gets irritable and hard to live with. Summer is the busiest time in the royal calendar and Prince Charles rushes about desperate to squeeze in games between his official commitments. Throughout the 1987 polo season he played more often than in any previous year with forty games in one ninety-day period, plus numerous practice sessions.

The concentration the game demands wipes everything else from his mind. It is a hazardous game for hard men and the Prince has been lucky to escape so far with a sprained wrist, a scar on his left cheek and a few bruises. The game also satisfies Charles' liking for a sense of danger. As he admits: 'I feel sheer terror but I also enjoy it tremendously.'

Perhaps because his life has always been so cosseted the Prince loves to risk his neck as often as possible. As he has explained: 'I am a hopeless individual because I happen to enjoy an element of danger. I think that if you occasionally live dangerously it helps you appreciate life.' He finds the same challenge riding to hounds in winter – which has the beneficial effect of improving his riding ability and thereby his polo.

He usually manages to find the time each winter for a week's break at the Swiss resort, Klosters. On one skiing trip he went over the lethal black run called the Wange, which many of the world's most experienced winter sports stars regard as the ultimat .est of courage.

The thrills and occasional spills he encounters outdoors provide a much-needed reprieve from the dull round of factory inspections, formal banquets and other royal duties. Without

16

these regular respites the Prince knows he simply could not cope.

His wife understands this too. The fact that she is so often waiting down by the pony lines when he finishes a game reveals a lot about the state of their relationship. What ordinary wife would put up with a husband who scooted off to play soccer or cricket as often as that? She would much rather watch a game of tennis or play a few sets herself. But she is there most Sunday afternoons dodging the occasional shower and braving the chill breezes of the typical English summer to watch her husband and his ponies work up a sweat.

When a Sunday newspaper ran the story about her husband and Fiammetta Frescobaldi, Diana silenced the gossips by turning up at the polo the same afternoon with both her children. Together they watched the Prince at his favourite sport, providing the perfect picture of a happy family. The following Sunday it was cold and rainy but the Princess was back at Smith's Lawn with her children again. It seemed an obvious way to show the world that they were united in their affection for each other.

Few people realise that she quite often follows Prince Charles when he goes foxhunting – although usually at some distance by car. In the winter of 1986–7 she also borrowed a hunter from her sister Lady Sarah McCorquodale and rode out with the Belvoir to gain a better understanding of his love of the hunt. It is an exhilarating experience to canter across green countryside but jumping fences and hedges takes nerve, stamina and skill. The Princess is definitely no goddess-like Diana the Huntress, but she gamely tackled some very testing fences with the Belvoir and didn't come off once.

Predictably, a storm erupted when news of this reached the press. A spokesman for the League Against Cruel Sports attacked the Princess for joining in and asked 'If she believes foxes are pests, and is acting as a mounted Rentokil officer'.

Well aware that many people have reservations about 'blood sports', Diana knew her appearance at any meet would bring criticism if it leaked out. That was precisely why she had gone hunting without her husband. Local journalists often follow him when he goes out with the Quorn or Belvoir, although they rarely pick up a story worth selling to Fleet Street.

Michael Clayton, the editor of *Horse and Hound*, says the Prince finds following the hounds for five or even six hours a day is a unique form of relaxation, 'for no telephone messages nor other official communications are possible in the hunting field'. In other words, hunting, like polo, is an ideal way to escape from the stress of his frustrating life.

An intriguing aspect of the Prince's passion for this sport is his unique hunting dress known as 'the Windsor Coat'. When he rides out Charles wears a dark blue jacket with scarlet collar and matching cuffs over white cord hunting breeches. Black boots with tan-trimmed tops and a very dark blue hunting cap add the finishing touches. This outfit was specially copied for him from a uniform favoured by King George III.

The Prince has always been fascinated by the king remembered in history as 'the Mad Monarch'. Once when asked which previous sovereign he would most wish to be like he immediately named this peculiar ancestor.

Charles always protests that George III was not really insane but a victim of a blood disease known as porphyria, which produced delirium and other symptoms of madness. The Prince was one of the first people to point out that the sad sovereign was actually a victim of the ignorance of his time. Later research revealed that the disease could be traced back through the royal house of Stuart to Mary Queen of Scots and her son James VI of Scotland.

King George was a much misunderstood monarch, which obviously inspires a fellow feeling in Prince Charles. He can never understand why his well-meaning attempts to do his best are so often misinterpreted by the press. 'I think he was a most wonderful man, a really great human being, wonderful with people,' he often says of his ancestor.

In his day the unhappy king, known to his subjects as 'Farmer George', received a lot of abuse from both the press and the people. His great-great-great-great-great-great-great

18

grandson Charles thinks that even today history treats the simple, plain-speaking king very shabbily.

Compassionate Charles is always ready to speak up for the underdog, even if he is sometimes ridiculed for doing so. But this time the Prince wanted to set the record straight because he knows mistaken ideas seem to spread more quickly than the truth. That is certainly true in his case. Ever since he mentioned in a television interview that he talked to his plants people have been asking if Charles is as dotty as a tiger lily.

But sometimes he himself adds fuel to the fire of this sort of speculation, as when he once astonished an audience in Canada with a mystical chat about 'inner peace'. The townsfolk of St George, British Columbia, sat stunned as he told them: 'I rather feel that deep in the soul of mankind there is a reflection as on the surface of a mirror or a mirror-calm lake, of the beauty and harmony of the universe. We must develop an awareness of this to attain inner peace and world peace.'

Even earlier, in a speech to the Mental Health Foundation of Australia in 1983 Prince Charles talked about the pressures of modern life and their emotional toll. His earnest delivery gave the impression that he spoke from personal knowledge of the subject. He pointed out that in Britain one in three people have some form of mental illness.

'There is clearly an enormous problem affecting Westernised man, which has been growing steadily in significance through-out this century,' he declared. The cause, he suggested, 'is that as modern man we have lost that sense of meaning within nature's scheme of things which helps to preserve that delicate balance between the world of the instinctive unconscious and that of the conscious.'

He went on to say obscurely: 'If we did but know it, so many of the things we feel, as it were unconsciously, are things we share, but which seem to become trapped within us through that fear of being thought different or odd.' He added that he knew what he was saying was rather confused but stressed the importance of getting in touch with the side of our being 'which cries out for recognition ... in other words the soul'.

But his heartfelt message did not seem to impress his audience of psychiatrists and psychoanalysts who had dined and wined lavishly before the Prince got up to speak.

Both speeches were courageous attempts to make people think about philosophical subjects, never an easy task. But revealing this sensitive, contemplative side of his character immediately made one man in the Canadian audience describe him as 'just plain loony'. Others complained his message went straight over their heads.

Back home in London these speeches labelled him as a true eccentric in reports headlined 'Guru Charles' and 'The Mystic Prince'. It certainly seemed, as an American critic argued, that Charles was a Yippie in an age of Yuppies.

Alone of all his royal relatives this Prince appears to be plagued by such deep concerns. He seeks to draw attention to, even if he can do nothing to solve, the problems of our society. But the more he tries the more it seems he is misunderstood. His 'inner peace' speech inspired TV send-ups poking fun at his barmy ideas. Central Television's 'Spitting Image' portrayed him meditating in a loin cloth, prattling to his plants and, in a sketch about spiritualism, declaring: 'I don't want people to think I've gone bananas.' To those who know him well it was no joke.

He was even more depressed when the media totally mis-understood his reasons for going off on a mystery trek into the Kalahari in March 1987. But it did look decidedly weird, as if the Prince was walking off into the wilderness with a mystic while his wife was dumped at home. That is, until one of the Prince's staff revealed that the Princess had originally been pencilled in to accompany her husband to Africa.

But once Diana saw the programme of factory tours, trips around dusty tea plantations and coffee shambas with not a minute to lie by a swimming pool, she decided it was not for her. The desert safari at the end of the tour was definitely *Boys' Own* adventure stuff too, so please include me out, Diana pleaded.

It would certainly have been no picnic for a pampered

princess. As Prince Charles relished telling me later: 'Although I didn't see a single lion they kept us awake when we tried to sleep. One came right into our camp one night but fortunately made off with only a plastic bucket. I couldn't imagine why a lion would fancy that but it must have tasted OK because we never saw the bucket again.

'There were a lot of scorpions too. We found a dead one when we got up one morning. It had obviously crawled out of some old, dried wood we had stacked up for the campfire. Without realising it, one of us had trodden on the thing and killed it. Not me, I assure you.'

The Prince's guide into the trackless Kalahari, Sir Laurens van der Post, dispelled any mystery about mystic mumbo-jumbo under the stars. Talking to me on the tarmac of Nairobi airport shortly before he flew off with Prince Charles to begin their trek he said: 'I'm taking the Prince to a place called Deception Pan because it is one of the loveliest places in Africa at this time of year. The rains have come to the Kalahari and the whole desert is blooming with wild flowers. It is a wonderful sight to see. But best of all there are no people anywhere. We'll be able to walk for miles without seeing a soul.'

Later one of the royal hiking party confirmed that there had been no time for the Prince to sit meditating in the desert with his guru. 'We were up and off by 5.30 each morning. We must have walked dozens of miles each day because my feet certainly felt like it. So at night we were all exhausted and went to bed very early.'

Then he added thoughtfully: 'But I must say the endless walking was well worth it. We saw some spectacular sights in the desert – not just the wild flowers but also some wonderful mirages that appeared and disappeared as we stared at the horizon. It always seemed that a huge expanse of water lay just ahead but, of course, it wasn't there at all, just a trick of the light. It was an eerie experience, but beautiful just the same.'

Yet the vast emptiness of this remote region clearly helped the Prince to refresh his mind. Away from the red-carpeted

21

world he knew too well, roughing it in tents, eating meals cooked on a campfire, and polishing his own boots, Prince Charles was in heaven. There were no phone calls, no hands to shake, no official reports to read and no speeches to write. He had escaped briefly from the burdens back home.

Perhaps this is the simple explanation for his repeated absences from Diana's side. Prince Charles has found a way to steal away not from his wife but from a life he sometimes loathes.

Less than a month later he disappeared from London again to spend three days without his family living with a crofter on the island of Berneray in the Hebrides. To earn his keep he planted potatoes, helped to build drystone walls and went fishing for his supper.

His retreat from the world yet again was simply his way of finding out how the islanders lived, explained a Buckingham Palace spokesman. It was all part of his education for the throne. But it was his fifth break from official life in four months, growing evidence of his preference for the simple life.

In 1983 and again in 1984 he had taken off to work as a farmhand on Duchy of Cornwall properties, milking cows, delivering calves and building stone fences. Afterwards he declared that the labour had been hard and his back hurt but he had gained a great sense of contentment.

'I think being here has restored my sanity,' he added significantly.

3

Early Days

A window flew open with a clatter and a fair head suddenly appeared looking out as Prince Charles climbed into a Range Rover outside Sandringham House.

'That's right, go and have lunch with your mother and leave me here all alone,' his angry wife yelled.

Her furious protest was almost loud enough to be heard at the Jubilee Gates of the royal estate 200 yards away. But ignoring this outburst Charles put his car into gear and drove off to join the Queen's shooting party in a picnic lunch.

Moments later Princess Diana rushed out of the house and roared off after him in her Ford Escort to continue the row. A few miles down the road she waved him down and forced him to pull over at the side of the road.

Startled beaters from the shoot saw her leap out of her car and dash over to the Range Rover as Charles wound his window down. Her face flushed with anger Diana yelled: 'Why do you do this to me? Why can't we just have a meal alone together for a change?'

News of the newlyweds' quarrel soon went right round Sandringham. The world's most famous couple had only been married six months and the new Princess was pregnant.

But this dramatic low in their relationship was counterbalanced by moments of great tenderness. Like any other newly married couple they were still learning to live with each other.

Charles' loving concern for his young wife was never more evident than when, a short time after their public row, she tripped and fell down the main staircase of Sandringham House.

He rushed to cradle her in his arms while calling urgently for staff to summon the local doctor. Happily, Diana and the baby she was carrying had both escaped any injury, but Charles insisted that she go to bed and stay there until the doctor gave her the all clear. He sat holding her hand and comforting her until the shock of her accident wore off.

The following year after the birth of their first son, Prince William, their headstrong personalities clashed repeatedly. They argued so often in front of strangers that a Palace press secretary once felt it necessary to warn a visitor to Kensington Palace. 'If they start a barney in front of you, please pretend you don't notice,' he pleaded.

The adjustment from single person to spouse was probably more difficult for Charles, who was very settled in his ways and dangerously close to becoming a crusty old bachelor when he met his wife.

Very few people, including Diana, realised this because to the world at large the Prince was best known then as the Royal Action Man. It seems hard to recall, now that he is renowned for nattering to his plants and strolling through the desert with a guru, but right through the Seventies Charles was portrayed in the press as a hairy-chested adventurer.

He had dived under the polar ice cap and commanded his own warship. He had flown supersonic Phantom and Nimrod jets on sorties out into the North Sea. He had even risked his neck with the Paras by leaping out of an Andover over Dorset when the wind speed was well above the RAF maximum strength for safe descents.

In rare moments off duty he was often photographed while locked in a torrid embrace with a gorgeous model or actress. Girls literally threw themselves at him everywhere he went.

No Hollywood heart-throb or rock star stud could offer any woman more. He was quite simply the world's most eligible bachelor, the catch of the century. This was the man that the naive teenager Diana Spencer had fallen for.

But after a wedding which naturally became a round-the-world satellite spectacular, Diana discovered that she was married not to this dashing ladykiller, but to a self-indulgent mother's boy who left her alone far too often.

Like a reversal of the Grimms' fairytale Diana soon realised she had kissed a prince only to see him turn into a frog. Perhaps it is not such a coincidence that she still has a frog mascot on the bonnet of her car, a gift of several years ago from Prince Andrew.

As it happens, Charles has a deep tinge of green right through. An ardent conservationist, he believes that organic farming is best for the environment. He works hard to persuade farmers on his Duchy of Cornwall properties to adopt his ideas although they are not always so profitable, and he also loves spending hours alone digging in his garden at Highgrove.

This dull, domestic scene was not what Diana had imagined life would be like with the world's most glamorous man. Her disappointment was shared by her first butler Alan Fisher. He had formerly worked in Hollywood, and soon left the Royal Household after claiming his job was 'boring' because the Waleses hardly ever entertained.

When still a schoolgirl Diana had dreamed of becoming Princess of Wales. One day her dream miraculously came true, but it turned out totally different from the one she had expected. Her Prince Charming was a much more serious fellow than he had been when they were secretly dating and the press were always in hot pursuit. Every day was an exciting adventure then. But marriage was not so much fun. Most of the time she was stuck away from her friends in the country with a lot of elderly people. It was a huge anti-climax.

Many people closely connected to the Royal Family had privately doubted that the union between the charming but immature Lady Diana Spencer and the sophisticated, solemn Prince could work out. Diana was barely twenty when she married on 29 July 1981 but Charles, who was thirty-two, seemed far older. As well as this yawning, twelve-and-a-half-year age gap, the couple seemed to have little in common, and a few of the Prince's oldest friends seemed concerned that the pair might not be at all compatible. He was a history graduate who enjoyed opera, art galleries and the conversation of deep thinkers while her main pastime seemed to be shopping, and a few evenings in her company convinced his cronies that nothing more weighty than a hefty account from Harrods had ever crossed her mind.

Everyone else seemed to notice only the links between Charles and Diana – her family had served his for centuries. She was literally the girl next door, growing up on the Sandringham estate at Park House, which her father, then Viscount Althorp and a former royal equerry, leased from the Queen.

She had always been tipped as a possible royal bride, although most people had mentally married her off to Prince Andrew, who was much closer to her in age and interests. 'I always used to gang up with Andrew,' Diana herself admitted afterwards.

The first time either Charles or Diana can recall meeting the other was in November 1977, when the Prince went to shoot at Althorp as her eldest sister Sarah's boyfriend. Diana, then sixteen, was home for the weekend from boarding school when she was introduced to Charles in the middle of a ploughed field near Nobottle Wood on the Spencer estate.

After meeting at Ascot, Charles and Sarah had been seeing each other regularly for months. Although touted as a possible bride she was never really more than a chum. Their friendship fizzled out after Sarah told a reporter: 'He is a fabulous person, but I am not in love with him ... our relationship is purely platonic.'

Despite denting his ego, Sarah remained friendly with Charles. And the Queen decided to invite her and Diana to Sandringham for a weekend in January 1979. From that time on the Prince and Sarah's little sister began to see quite a lot of each other.

She was not his girlfriend, just another attractive girl invited to make up a group on outings to dinner and the theatre. Gradually Charles found he began to enjoy her lively company more and more.

In the summer of 1980 Prince Charles was on the rebound from a disastrous romance with a very beautiful but demanding blonde called Anna Wallace. The daughter of a Scottish landowner she was nicknamed 'Whiplash' because of her love of hunting, a passion the Prince also shared.

He dated her for almost a year until they had a row when he escorted her to a ball in honour of the Queen Mother's eightieth birthday in August 1980. While Charles circulated among the 250 guests all night Anna decided she was being ignored when he failed to return to her side. Finally, she stormed out after telling the Prince in a loud voice: 'I've never been so badly treated before in my life.' As he tried to splutter an explanation Anna lashed out again: 'No one treats me like that – not even you.' Exit Miss Wallace and enter Lady Diana.

The very same month that Anna Wallace walked out of his life Diana Spencer had been Prince Charles' guest aboard the Royal Yacht *Britannia* during Cowes Week. But her name did not appear on the passenger list and the ship's photographer, who snapped every guest as they came aboard, did not know she was in the royal party. The tall blonde was smuggled on to the ship in great secrecy. The few people who did spot her thought she was with Prince Edward.

It was not until 8 September 1980 that Diana's name was publicly linked with Charles'. The Prince had spent the previous weekend with the then unknown blonde at Balmoral in the Scottish Highlands. The *Sun*'s sharp-eyed royal photographer, Arthur Edwards, had spotted her disguised in waders, bulky Barbour coat and cap, watching from the riverbank as Prince Charles fished in the River Dee.

Another guest at Balmoral that weekend passed on the information that the mystery girl's name was Lady Diana Spencer. The informant added that she was so potty about the Prince that she had followed him around everywhere 'like a little lamb'.

Some months earlier Arthur Edwards had noticed the leggy teenager at a polo match enthusiastically supporting Les Diables Bleus (the Blue Devils team for which the Prince was playing) at Midhurst, Sussex. When he learned who she was he had banged off a shot of her sitting in the private members' enclosure 'just in case'. When she realised his camera was focused on her she had blushed a deep scarlet and an alarm bell went off in his newsman's brain.

Although the photographer did not know it then Diana Spencer was the Prince's guest at the match. Charles drove off afterwards in his Aston Martin without so much as a glance in her direction. But they met up afterwards at the nearby home of his old friend Robert de Pass. They had spent the weekend there together.

The couple were beginning to realise that their casual relationship was turning into something stronger when Diana flew up to Balmoral to join Charles once again. The story of the Prince's new love affair was announced to the world with the headline 'He's in love again. Lady Di is the new girl for Charles.'

The Prince had been attracted to her at first because she was wonderfully good-looking and great fun. He had always fancied bosomy blondes and Diana Spencer, with her peachy complexion and curvy figure, was as alluring as any of the worldly females he had been involved with in the past. She was also strikingly stylish and tall, and the Prince liked women who were on his level.

Earl Spencer's youngest daughter seemed to be his ideal woman. But she also had another irresistible plus. She was fresh and unspoiled. Her untarnished reputation was essential for the role of future queen. Her youth also meant that she was perfect for the job of producing heirs to the throne, since the best years for a woman to give her husband healthy children are supposed to be in her early twenties. And Diana's sharp, irreverent wit made him laugh. He felt relaxed and happy in her company. But was he madly in love when he proposed marriage?

Most Fleet Street royal reporters at the time doubted it. They based their conclusions on statements made by Charles himself. They recalled that the Prince had once declared how he would set about choosing a wife. 'If I'm deciding on whom I want to live with for the next fifty years – well, that's the last decision in which I'd want my head to be ruled entirely by my heart,' he said.

'You have to remember that when you marry in my position, you're going to marry someone who, perhaps, is one day going to be queen. You've got to choose somebody very carefully, I think, who could fulfil this particular role, and it has got to be somebody pretty unusual.'

Obviously he was looking for a woman who would be right for the job as his consort first, and a person he could love second. And he was terrified, he confided to an aide, of getting it wrong.

When speculation about his relationship with Lady Diana was at its height Charles seemed unsure of his feelings and didn't want anyone to rush him. 'If only I could live with a girl before marrying her,' said Charles to a group of royal correspondents. 'But I can't. It's all right for chaps like you. You can afford to make a mistake, but I've got to get it right first time. And if I get it wrong, you will be the first to criticise me in a few years' time.'

Was Diana the girl who could meet all the requirements of a future queen? It was definitely 'Make-Your-Mind-Up' time for Charles when he ended his visit to the Subcontinent with a trek into the serene atmosphere of the Himalayas. After flying home from India, Charles told his parents that he was on the point of proposing. To banish any lingering doubts he needed more time alone with her. His mother agreed that Diana should join them for the New Year holiday at Sandringham so her son could finally decide if she was the girl he really wanted.

The Duke of Edinburgh had been grumbling for some time that if his son didn't hurry up and choose a wife there would be no nice girls left. He was also concerned that while Charles wrestled with the greatest problem he had ever faced, he was being unfair to the girl who waited for his decision.

The long list of lovelies that Charles had loved and left was fast becoming a joke. The Queen's subjects were beginning to tire of this endless search for the right girl. And behind closed Palace doors there were muttered comparisons with the late Duke of Windsor who, when he was Prince of Wales, failed to find a suitable, single girl, fell in love with a married woman and shook the throne to its foundations.

Like everyone else around him the Queen, too, was anxious that he should make his mind up one way or another, and not only because she wanted Charles to produce an heir and guarantee the line of succession. The whole family had been living under seige from the press while Charles dallied over his decision. 'The idea of this romance going on for another year is intolerable for everyone concerned,' his mother declared.

With pressures mounting from all sides Charles had very little time to make the most important decision of his life. The whole world approved of Diana and thought she was the perfect choice to be his Princess. Everyone, from Palace kitchen maids to Fleet Street editors, was asking: 'Why doesn't he just get on with it and make an announcement?'

Shortly before Diana left for a visit to her mother's farm in Australia Charles decided to propose. 'I wanted to give Diana a chance to think about it – to think if it all was going to be too awful. She'd planned to go to Australia with her mother quite a long time before anyway, and I thought, "Well, I'll ask her then so that she'll have a chance of thinking it over while she's away, so she can decide if she can bear the whole idea – or not, as the case may be."'

But Diana did not need time to think. She was absolutely sure that she wanted to marry Charles. Her teenage dream to capture the heart of a prince was all coming true. Even when Charles pointed out the loneliness, the lack of privacy, and other problems of life at Court then urged her to think things over, she never wavered. 'It's what I want,' she said firmly.

After months of dashing about the country, dodging cameramen who tried to catch them together, the Prince and his fiancée faced the world together for the first time on the morning of their engagement. During a television interview they were asked if they were in love. While Diana at once sighed happily and declared: 'Of course,' the Prince hedged. 'Whatever "in love" means,' he added cagily.

Years afterwards she admitted that when a naive nineteen-year-old she simply did not know what she was letting herself in for. She described the experience to a fellow guest at a charity lunch in 1985: 'One day I was riding to work on a Number 9 bus, then suddenly all this happened.' And with a sweep of one hand she indicated her elevated position at the top table under the relentless scrutiny of the crowded room.

But caught up in the celebrations and preparations for her wedding, Diana had little time to consider what lay ahead. After all, princesses in storybooks always live happily ever after and this was the fairytale romance to end them all. Everyone said so.

Charles had proposed marriage to a carefree teenager, not too different from a million other London working girls except that her dad was an Earl. Now he expected her to throw off her happy-go-lucky life as easily as she tossed aside her flounced cotton dresses. Like a modern Cinderella, she had to leap out of a lowly kindergarten assistant's clogs, pop on glass slippers and become a glittering fairytale princess locked away from the real world.

At first, it had seemed gorgeous Lady Di could cope with her new life without batting one beautiful blue eye. Prince Charles was convinced that the transformation was complete the night in March 1981 shortly after their betrothal when he escorted her to their first joint engagement at the Goldsmiths' Hall in London.

For some reason best known to Diana and her dress designers she decided to break a royal rule and wear black, a colour royals wear only for mourning. But Charles did not even notice this breach of protocol when she waltzed into his sitting room at Buckingham Palace and twirled around the room to show off her new gown. It was a low-cut, strapless design that revealed a daring cleavage. Prince Charles' late valet Stephen Barry remembered the devastating effect she had on him when she arrived. The only word Barry could summon up was an awe-struck 'Gosh!'

Like everyone who saw her that night Charles, too, thought she looked breathtaking. As he stepped out of his car at the Goldsmiths' Hall he could not help bragging about the stunning beauty in his wake. 'Wait until you see what's coming next,' he announced to the pressmen crowding around the door.

To avoid bumping her head on the car door frame as she stepped out Diana bent so low that she exposed a real royal eyeful. Spectators in the crowd asked each other if they had really seen what they thought they had. And reporters went rushing to telephones to file stories about 'The night Lady Di almost made an amazing boob'.

Later that evening the 'News at Ten' production team held a crisis meeting to decide the correct way to screen the titillating footage they had filmed. Finally, in a departure from their normally reverent reporting on the Queen's family, ITN asked if Di's daring décolletage had slipped below the point of decency. It seemed that the demure kindergarten helper who blushed furiously just a few months before when caught by cameramen in a see-through skirt had vanished. In her place had appeared a woman who could wow the world.

But the strain of this transition began to show now and then. Even before her wedding Diana discovered the acute discomfort of being the globe's most gawked-at celebrity. Just days before she was due to walk down the aisle she burst into tears and ran off when crowds pressed in too close at a polo match in Hampshire. This lapse from her normally cheery nature worried Prince Charles. Was she really the right person to cope with the demanding role of future queen? Had she cracked up totally with just five days to go before the wedding? But Diana soon perked up, began to enjoy herself once again and his fears evaporated.

It was an enormous shock for her to discover once she was whisked inside Palace walls what the rest of her life was going to be like. One of Princess Margaret's friends perfectly summed up the boredom of mixing with royalty on a regular basis. 'What do the Queen's family do all day?' he was asked.

'The same as everyone else,' he replied. 'Except in a slower, grander, duller way.'

From the day she became Princess of Wales, Diana found that her husband's family expected her to give up almost all personal freedom and adopt the stern obligations of her royal position. When Diana and Charles returned from a blissful two-week honeymoon cruise around the Mediterranean he took her to Balmoral where the Queen was spending her annual summer holiday. Living under the watchful eye of her mother-in-law would hardly thrill any young bride. And Diana soon discovered that she had to fall into line with traditional customs at Court or pay the penalty.

One of her first mistakes was to grow bored when dinners attended by many elderly royal officials and other not-so-young guests dragged on for hours. The Queen frowned when Diana, never a hearty eater, picked at her meal then urged her husband to leave his place at the table to watch television or go for a walk. 'If you can't endure an ordinary family dinner I simply don't know how you're going to cope at banquets,' the Queen said.

When Charles refused to leave the dining room with her, Diana left her seat to throw herself into his lap. With her arms around his neck she playfully planted kisses all over his face. But onlookers tut-tutted about this wifely display of affection and considered her behaviour 'bad form'.

Diana found herself irritated by stuffy royal rules and could not get used to the idea of other people doing things that she had always done for herself. She raised eyebrows when older staff members dropped something and she instinctively stooped to pick it up for them. And on another occasion at a dinner party she quietly left the room when it was time to leave and reappeared at the door with her coat over her arm. It had not occurred to her to ask anyone else to get it. Another time, she disappeared during dinner and her hostess later found her up to her elbows at the kitchen sink doing the dishes. The new Princess seemed to be desperately seeking the normal life she had so willingly given up.

Royal advisers predicted the frenzied coverage of the future queen would die away after the royal couple married and settled down. The Queen's press secretary, Michael Shea, later admitted they were wrong. 'We expected that, following the honeymoon, press attention would wane somewhat, but it has in no way abated,' he said. 'The Princess of Wales feels totally beleaguered. The people who love and care for her are anxious at the effect it is having.'

Interest in the new royal sweetheart developed into a stampede for news about her all over the world. Then three months after the wedding of the century she delighted everyone again with the announcement that she was expecting a baby. The girl was such good news the media just could not get enough of her.

But while Diana was trying to cope with suddenly becoming a British phenomenon bigger than the Beatles at their best she had another problem. The royal bride was starting to realise just what she had given up when she married her prince: she couldn't go anywhere alone any longer – for security reasons a Scotland Yard police officer remained at her elbow wherever she went. She had to watch what she said constantly for fear of offending any of the Queen's subjects and a million other minor restrictions were suddenly imposed on her. These ranged from being forced to wear hats on royal occasions – she had never even owned any sort of headgear before – to driving only British cars because royals must always 'fly the flag'.

Three young women were assigned to her as ladies-in-waiting: Anne Beckwith-Smith, who was to work full-time for the Princess, and Hazel West and Lavinia Baring who were to help out part-time. But Diana was not allowed to select these close companions. They were carefully chosen by the Queen's ladies and approved by Her Majesty. Slowly the new Princess began to realise that she could do very little without her mother-in-law's say-so.

She spent her first Christmas as a married woman with her husband's family and any idea that she might in turn spend the next with her own relatives at Althorp was firmly ruled out. Prince Charles had always enjoyed the festive season with his mother at Windsor: it was the Queen's wish that her children would gather together on every important holiday.

Heavy hints were also dropped that Diana might make more of an effort to join in the Queen's off-duty pleasures. 'She was never told she had to go riding with the Queen,' explains someone close to the Royal Household. 'She was simply asked if she was going to give it a try. Diana could not very well refuse without appearing to be rude. She couldn't even beg off because she lacked riding clothes. Every royal home has stacks of gear so the Princess had to give in. Fortunately, after one or two outings on horseback she became pregnant and was excused from further rides.'

Even before the age of nine, when she had fallen from her pony Romany, Diana had been a reluctant rider. Mary Clarke, a sensible Norfolk girl, was the Spencer nanny at the time. She remembers that the family doctor found nothing wrong when he examined the little girl, and two days later Diana went off on a skiing holiday with her mother. When she came home her arm was in a sling. Diana said she had fractured it in the riding fall. Afterwards the accident became her excuse for refusing offers to go riding. But it simply was not on to turn down a royal command to saddle up – another pressure to add to the ones that were piling up on Diana.

Throughout the early days of her marriage the Queen sympathised with her daughter-in-law's struggle to adjust to a strange new life. 'She is not like the rest of us,' the Queen explained when Di's antics astonished her in-laws. 'She wasn't born into our way of life.' The concerned mother-in-law even called Fleet Street editors together in an unprecedented plea to give her son's wife more privacy.

It was certainly not the Queen as a person who annoyed Diana then, but the petty restrictions of life at Court over which the Queen presided. Apart from Christmas and Easter at Windsor, Diana had no option but to spend New Year at Sandringham, as well as the August summer holidays at Balmoral. This was what the Queen wanted, therefore it was what her devoted son Charles wanted too.

The birth of Charles and Diana's first child Prince William created more conflicts with the Queen, who considered an heir to the throne should be born in the protected surroundings of Buckingham Palace as her own children had been. Diana, backed by her gynaecologist Mr George Pinker, was adamant that for safety reasons her baby would arrive in a modern, well-equipped hospital. And she got her way.

Clashes between the two women continued when Diana's first Commonwealth tour of Australia and New Zealand was planned. Royal advisers assumed that the Princess would leave her young baby behind when she went off around the world. Diana refused to consider it. She was reminded that personal sacrifices had to be made in the line of duty and aides cited the example of the Queen who left Prince Charles when he was tiny to tour Canada. But Diana would not budge. The extra expense and preparation required to house a royal infant did not impress her.

Meanwhile, the Prince of Wales' staff went ahead with arrangements that did not include a nine-month-old baby. Palace sources leaked to the press the news that the Princess would simply have to grit her teeth and get on with the job without her son.

In despair Diana issued an ultimatum to her husband. 'If William's not going, I'm not going. And that's final.' Miraculously, a plan was immediately put forward to base the baby and his nanny Barbara Barnes at a country homestead called Woomargama in Victoria, while his parents flew in and out on official duties. Diana had won the battle but she discovered afterwards that she had lost the war. William and his little brother Harry have never joined their parents during a tour since then.

The friction between Britain's two most famous women soon began to trouble Prince Charles. He has always worshipped his mother and worries that he will never be able to equal her achievements as sovereign. Increasingly he sided with his mother when she disagreed with his wife.

Some of the friction was, as some said, caused by the fact that it was a new and disturbing experience for the Queen to be downgraded from star of the royal show to a supporting player. For more than thirty years she had been the first lady in the land. Suddenly a younger, prettier woman had replaced her in the hearts of the nation. Her understandable feeling of resentment was glimpsed when photographers constantly swarmed around the Princess of Wales while ignoring her. It happened every time the Queen and Diana appeared in public together. 'I suppose I'd better get out of the way,' the Queen declared in an icy tone as shutters clicked and motor-drives whirred when she and her daughter-in-law arrived together at a Windsor polo match.

Diana noticed her mother-in-law's irritation but felt there was not much she could do about it. If she lowered her head and did not give the photographers a dazzling smile the newspapers attacked her next day for being moody or uncooperative. When she tried to discuss the problem with her husband he was most unsympathetic. He had also noticed that his beautiful wife grabbed more attention than he did. Although proud that she was so popular and the public clearly approved of his choice, he got a bit huffy when she was cheered more loudly than he was.

Several other leading personalities in the family, accustomed to hitting the headlines regularly, suddenly realised they were being ignored. The new star in the royal roadshow was outshining all the old performers who usually topped the bill.

'If you think about it you will realise that you very rarely see the entire royal family together at one time,' observes a man close to the Royal Household. 'It has to be a very special event such as a birthday or funeral to attract the lot. This is because they do not like sharing the limelight. They always protest that they hate being harassed by the press, but privately they love seeing their photographs in the newspapers. I once saw Princess

Anne zoom out of a royal estate in her car straight past a crowd of photographers at the gates. Not one camera was aimed in her direction so she drove around to the back entrance and a few minutes later crept through the gates again in low gear so that all the pressmen could get a clear shot. She used to do that a lot when all the reporters and photographers were chasing Lady Diana Spencer. I reckon she was just jealous. Most of the family are exactly the same. The only one who really couldn't give a damn if his face never appeared on a front page again is the Duke of Edinburgh.'

Diana had at first appeared to be the answer to the Royal Family's prayers. But when she became more popular with the public than they had ever dreamed her husband's relatives were a little miffed.

Until he found a wife, Charles was far closer to his mother than most men his age. A bachelor in his thirties who still lived at home with his parents, he never went out in the evening without first calling to wish the Queen goodnight. With the exception of a short annual skiing trip he spent all his holidays with her. He shared her passion for country life and dedication to the family firm. Instinctively shy and solemn like his mother, Charles forced himself by a tremendous effort of will to become more outgoing as his mother had done. Their unique destiny created a very special bond between them.

This cosy situation abruptly changed once he had a wife. Prince Charles' devotion to his mother was to become the reason for a succession of rows with his wife in the years ahead. It was probably inevitable that the Queen and her daughter-in-law Diana would not get along very well. They are such wildly different characters. The Queen, an older sister, was brought up to dedicate her life to duty. Diana, the youngest of three sisters – with only one younger brother – was her father's spoiled darling and until she married into the Royal Family she had always done exactly as she pleased.

Experts on the effects of stress claim that any change in a person's life, happy or sad, is a strain. And in less than a year the new Princess of Wales had undergone a greater transformation than most ordinary women experience in a lifetime: she had become engaged, married and pregnant all within nine short months; she had given up a job she loved for a far more responsible one; and then there was the unsettling experience of living in four different homes within the same year. These had consisted of her bachelor-girl flat at Coleherne Court, west London, which she moved out of after her engagement to stay briefly with the Queen Mother, at Clarence House, then she occupied a suite of rooms adjoining Prince Charles' in Buckingham Palace until her wedding. After the honeymoon Diana moved into Highgrove House, Charles' country home in Gloucestershire, while their London apartment at Kensington Palace was redecorated.

And on top of all this, Diana was slowly learning to cope with sudden superstardom. It was all a bit much for a girl who had not yet celebrated her twenty-first birthday.

When Charles took his bride off to Norfolk for a shooting party the following winter Diana was spotted running off through the shrubbery surrounding Sandringham House. She was heading for Park House, a rundown Victorian building next door to the royal residence. It was here that she was born, late in the evening of 1 July 1961. She lived in this spacious ten-bedroom house until her father inherited an earldom in 1975, when Diana was fourteen, and moved his family to the Spencer stately home, Althorp in Northamptonshire.

Although Park House looked cold and bleak with its boarded-up windows and closed shutters when she returned, the Princess remembered it as her only real home, the one place she had felt safe and secure.

In the autumn of 1967 Diana's mother Frances had walked out after years of unhappiness with Johnnie Spencer and in 1969 they were divorced. But her father tried hard to make up for the loss of her mother. He took his children to school and picked them up again each afternoon as often as he could. He fussed about them on rainy days, made them wear their wellies and warm coats. He kept in touch with their teachers and knew all their friends. Gradually, he restored the calm, cosy life the children had always known at Park House.

Hidden from the road by tall trees and flowering shrubs it had sheltered her when she had been nobody special, just a happy little girl who rode her bicycle around the garden and showed off by diving into the outdoor swimming pool.

It was only yards from the splendours of Sandringham House where Diana now belonged as Princess of Wales. But it might have been in another country. The two homes, almost side by side, symbolised the old, free life she had left forever and the stifling world of pomp and circumstance she had married into.

Eventually the Queen decided the neglected building deserved a new lease of life and handed it over it to the Leonard Cheshire Foundation who turned it into a three-star home for disabled people. It was officially opened in July 1987.

During the renovations Diana made several secret trips to see her old home before the interior became unrecognisable. Workmen salvaged a sash window from her old nursery, which had telephone numbers and friends' names scratched on its glass by the Princess when she was small, and sent it to her as a souvenir.

When she returned to Park House she never drove the long way round from Sandringham down the public road and into its gravelled drive. She always slipped away through the grounds of the royal estate, and forced a way through the dense foliage until she reached a high brick wall between the two properties.

Then she would look for toeholds in the crumbling mortar between the bricks and scramble over the wall into the grounds of Park House and dash across the cricket pitch the way she had done as a little girl. Undisturbed, the lonely figure of the Princess would wander around the dank, dusty rooms the workmen had not yet touched, as if in search of something she had lost.

4

A Prince at Work

A Fleet Street photographer stood glumly to one side as Prince Charles paused to inspect a machine twisting strands of nylon filament into twine. On the second day of an official visit to Malawi HRH the Prince of Wales was touring a factory making nylon fishing nets.

As the Prince drew near to the pressman they briefly exchanged glances. The photographer, well known to Charles for more than ten years, rolled his eyes up to heaven and placed a hand over his mouth as if stifling a yawn. Charles grinned at him then turned back with a completely straight face to the factory manager who was explaining the complicated process by which granular polypropylene is turned into twine for ropes. Doing his best to look enthralled the Prince commented: 'I see, how very interesting.'

Minutes earlier as his grey Daimler drew up outside the factory thousands of chanting local women swaying to the pulse-pounding rhythms of African drums lined the streets. The Mbumba women of Malawi turn out to dance and sing a greeting wherever their revered leader President Hastings Banda appears. To give Prince Charles the same welcome to the country known as The Warm Heart of Africa was a mark of their high regard for the British Queen's heir. But as he stepped out of the car Charles had only a brief glimpse of the Mbumba in their vivid tribal dress before the manager of the Blantyre Netting Company led him inside.

And the moment he walked through the door he might easily have been back home touring a similar plant in Barnsley or Leeds. The wild wailing of the African women outside was drowned by the noise of weaving looms and winding machinery. The British photographer sighed. Any pictures of this boring job were not even worth wiring back to London. The machine attendants kept their eyes down as if working normally, pretending they were unaware of the royal visitor and the scramble of officials and press following in his wake.

As he followed the factory manager through the raw material store the stench of stored cotton bales filled the building. The temperature was in the high eighties (hovering near the 30 degree Celsius mark) and in his light grey woollen suit the Prince looked uncomfortably warm. He might have preferred to wear a casual, open-necked safari jacket and slacks more appropriate for the tropical climate. But his valet Michael Fawcett had laid out city suit, shirt and tie because the Prince was driving straight on to an official meeting with President Banda after his factory tour.

Despite the sweltering atmosphere sweating African news-paper photographers pressed around Prince Charles on all sides every time he stopped to inspect any piece of machinery. Ignoring the blitz of flashguns inches away from his face, he concentrated keenly on everything shown to him.

'What goes on here, then?' he asked as he approached another mystifying array of clattering shuttles. For a minute or two every answer had his total attention, in a way so flattering and intense it just had to be a special royal technique. He kept nodding and smiling as his hosts tried to explain their production methods over the deafening roar of the machinery.

Contrary to most people's belief Prince Charles' daily life is more grind than glamour. For every star-studded film première he attends the Prince tours at least twenty factories or small businesses like this one in Blantyre, Malawi. For every slinky actress flashing perfectly capped teeth at him, he shakes hands with a hundred faceless executives.

It no doubt requires a great effort of will to appear interested, let alone fascinated, by many of them, especially when he is often dragged around by managements over-anxious to impress on him every tiny, tedious detail of their organisations. In twenty years of public life he has probably learned more about the world's more boring jobs than any other man is ever likely to. But this is his life. To his credit the Prince of Wales appears to make the most of it.

His visit to Malawi, a long, narrow sliver of a country between Zambia and Mozambique, was actually a business trip. As a board member of the Commonwealth Development Corporation since 1979 he was seeing for himself the way in which the flow of investment from Britain was helping to develop one small nation's economy.

The CDC was started in 1948 so that older, developed countries could lend money and expertise to newly emerging, under-developed ones and both could make a profit.

'We are not an aid organisation,' the CDC Chairman Lord Kindersley, had explained earlier as he stood in the scorching sun waiting for Prince Charles. 'We get a little bit of money from the British Government but we have to pay it back. That's good because it makes us very businesslike. The main part of our money comes from profits we make on our investments. For any of the services we provide we charge a fee. And when the company we have backed becomes viable we take out our money and start again somewhere else.'

Charles believes this is a worthy way to assist Commonwealth countries. 'The Prince enjoys being involved so much with this Commonwealth crusade,' added Lord Kindersley. 'He wants to preserve and protect it as his mother has always tried to do, so it is of deep concern to him what goes on out here.'

In Malawi the Corporation has £50 million invested in more than twenty projects which employ 22,795 people. At the factory in Blantyre the Prince was meeting a few of them.

In sharp contrast to the heat and exotic surroundings of Africa only days earlier on a bright but savagely cold winter morning the Prince's job took him to Finsbury Park, north London.

As his Jaguar drew up to the kerb outside a Muslim Welfare Centre and the car door opened, a long plume of his breath vaporised in the cold air. After meeting local Muslim community leaders in a gutted Victorian house, he walked out to inspect the site of a new mosque next door, which was then just a hole in the ground.

Through a gap in a fence around the property Charles stared at a sea of frozen mud with an abandoned earth-digger sitting on top. Shoving his hands deep into the pockets of a calf-length tweed overcoat to keep warm, he managed to look fascinated by the boggy crater for nine minutes. And all the while he kept up a flow of questions about the planned foundations, materials and construction methods.

From this site he had to drive around the corner to visit a run-down Bingo hall, then on to another excavation where derelict land was being reclaimed for an Afro-Caribbean project. But as he headed for his car he noticed a small bedraggled group of people huddled together behind a barrier across the road.

Walking over to them he asked: 'Will you use this mosque when it opens?' A girl wearing an overcoat over a sari spoke up. 'No, not me. I'm not a Muslim.' Turning to a grey-haired woman and her husband Charles tried again: 'Do you live around here?' The couple looked surprised. 'No, we've just driven down this morning from Northampton,' the woman explained. 'We only stopped when we noticed all the police cars to see what was going on.'

Usually, Prince Charles can talk to anyone about anything. It is a rare occasion when his friendly attempts to strike up a conversation with strangers fail to take off. But this was one of those days. The rest of the crowd were too tongue-tied to respond to his overtures.

He got luckier ninety minutes later when he attended a buffet lunch at the Jack Ashley Centre nearby. As President of Business in the Community he was meeting representatives from the local Islington, Hackney and Haringey Councils as well as the chairmen of eleven different major national companies.

A more powerful or influential group has probably never trod those decaying streets before. They included Sir Robert Reid, the Chairman of British Rail, concerned because BR land would be vital for the area's development, John Quinton, the Deputy Chairman of Barclays Bank, and Terry Heiser, Permanent Secretary at the Department of the Environment. Bernie Grant, then the controversial leader of Haringey Council, also met the Prince as well as representatives from the other two local authorities. These councillors, bankers, directors and other chief executives had come to see how their organisations might find ways to get involved in improving one of Britain's blighted areas.

Leaving their company limos behind, the sleek, successful bosses from the world of big business had all climbed aboard a mini-bus, like children on a school outing, so they could follow the Prince around Finsbury Park. They had found the time in their busy working weeks to be good neighbours to their customers, many unemployed, in an area of neglect.

It would be difficult to think of anyone other than the caring Prince who could have lured them all to the meeting. Charles passionately believes in the need to improve life in Britain's rundown inner cities. Business in the Community is, he reckons, the best way devised so far to do this and it has become his private crusade. He devotes long hours at his desk to promoting its aims and if Finsbury Park is an example, his hard graft is paying off.

As the lunch guests tucked into a delicious West Indian meal provided by a local firm originally set up with BIC help, they had plenty to discuss with the Prince of Wales. Even the left-winger Frances Morrell, then leader of the Inner London Education Authority, glowed when he spotted her well-known face just inside the door and sought her out for a chat. Later Ms Morrell explained a little defensively that naturally she had enjoyed talking to the Prince because 'he seems genuinely concerned about the problems in this area'.

After making a short speech in which he revealed he had secretly visited the borough's down-and-outs, Charles left an hour later at 2.30 p.m. without managing to swallow more than half a glass of orange juice. He had been too busy talking to sample the spicy chicken and rice salad on the menu.

During his visit he had announced that his old friend, American oil mogul Dr Armand Hammer had donated £25,000 to fund BIC projects in the Finsbury Park area. As he said his goodbyes the Prince noticed Sir Ranulf Fiennes, who works for Dr Hammer, standing to one side. 'Have you got the cheque yet, Ran?' Charles asked him. 'No, but I'll get on to it as soon as I get back to the office,' Fiennes promised. The Prince looked satisfied: 'You know they need the money here as soon as possible.'

He had left home at 8.30 that morning so that he could visit a new Barrett housing estate with special provision for handicapped residents in the East End of London before going on to Finsbury Park. His Jaguar purred back inside the gates of Kensington Palace at almost fifteen minutes past three o'clock.

An often quoted story about Prince Charles involves a Qantas air stewardess who once said to him at the end of a tour: 'What a rotten boring job you've got!' Instead of being offended the Prince immediately agreed with her. 'You don't understand, she was right!' he told friends afterwards.

Charles attends around 250 public engagements each year. These range from inspecting regiments and industrial plants, to attending receptions and making speeches, all of which he writes himself. An average of five jobs a week hardly seems a taxing schedule. But this official programme is only the visible tip of his workload – a fact few people appreciate.

Fleet Street's royal correspondents believe Charles' life is a cushy number. They point out that he plays polo more often than he does anything else. In 1987 he had more matches than ever before, playing as often as five or even six days a week including Saturdays and Sundays.

'You can tell polo is his number one priority,' says one dis-illusioned reporter, 'because Major Ronald Ferguson, his polo manager, attends all the planning meetings when his schedule is mapped out six months in advance. You can't blame anyone for believing Charles is a layabout when it seems that his work has to fit in with his favourite sport, not the other way round.'

Royal aide Lieutenant Commander Richard Aylard responds to this with the benefit of an insider's information. 'What the press don't realise is that immediately after he gets home from playing polo the Prince has a shower then sits down with a pile of official papers this high, he says raising one hand to indicate chest height.

'It doesn't matter whether it is Saturday, Sunday or any other day, there is always an enormous stack of work waiting for him. You should see the bags of papers that follow him around the world. I'm not just talking about Cabinet papers, but correspondence and reports from all the countless organis- ations the Prince is involved with like BIC and the United World Colleges to mention only two out of the 200 he heads.

'The Prince of Wales refuses to become a patron or president of anything unless he can be actively involved with it. He wants to do something to help, to be of use. As a result he often sits up until 2 a.m. reading and digesting all the paperwork that goes with his job.' Even at the 1987 Derby he sat in the back of the royal box working on government papers. 'If I don't do it now, when can I do it?' he explained.

From one organisation alone, the Commonwealth Develop- ment Corporation, the Prince gets literally thousands of papers each year. They are not just glanced at or filed away to be forgotten. He reads every one of them and if there is a single paragraph he is not clear about or which prompts a question he picks up the telephone to speak to the CDC main head- quarters in London. Because he has visited most Common- wealth countries the Prince can bring first-hand knowledge of many areas to some of the problems the organisation faces.

He also attends board meetings three or four times a year, or if other official duties prevent him attending personally, he sends his Private Secretary Sir John Riddell in his place.

'It isn't very exciting to pore through these reports all night,' says Richard Aylard. 'But it has to be done, so he gets on with it. The trouble is no one sees him sitting at his desk until well after midnight. The public don't know that before he goes off late in the afternoon to play polo he has already had a long list of appointments at home.

'His first meeting may be soon after nine o'clock in the morning. He sees people like the colonels of his regiments, officials from the Duchy of Cornwall and the Prince's Trust, as well as businessmen, charity organisers and hundreds of other leaders from various walks of life.

'Usually, he invites more officials or charity workers to a working lunch. None of this gets reported in the press, of course. For a start, it's not exciting enough to make headlines. And secondly, it is not listed on the Prince's official programme of engagements, so no one knows about it.'

An average day for the Prince begins at 6.30 a.m. when he gets up and has a shower. After breakfast with his wife and children he is often well underway with the day's work before eight o'clock sitting at his cluttered, antique desk in a study on the first floor of his London home.

He keeps up a huge volume of correspondence with people all over the world. Letters to close friends and relatives are often handwritten to ensure privacy or as a mark of his special regard.

Despite his long working day, royal observers argue that the Prince gets well paid for it. His income after tax from the Duchy of Cornwall was £1 million in 1986. And he gets plenty of time to put his feet up. He normally takes off about ten weeks each year.

In 1986 as well as his usual break at Sandringham over the New Year holiday, he went skiing in Switzerland for a week in January, flew off twice to sketch the scenery in Italy, took his family to Majorca for a week in August. He then returned before his wife and sons to join his mother aboard the *Britannia* as she sailed up to Scotland for her summer holiday at Balmoral, where he stayed more than three weeks.

In 1987 he returned to Italy for another week in the spring, he spent four days walking in the Kalahari desert with his friend and adviser Sir Laurens van der Post and also took his family to the Spanish resort Majorca once again in August. These breaks abroad were on top of his usual Christmas, Easter and summer holidays at home on the royal estates.

As well as time off to play polo from early May to late August he goes hunting every winter, a private passion which is not often publicised. His country home Highgrove lies in the heart of the Beaufort Hunt country and he normally manages a day out with them or the Quorn in Leicestershire twice a week.

On balance, it would not seem that Prince Charles is over-worked. His sister Princess Anne carries out around four hundred engagements each year, and she takes far fewer holidays.

'Ah, but Princess Anne does not get really into her jobs the way the Prince of Wales does,' argues a member of Charles' staff. 'She just goes through the motions, whereas he gets genuinely involved with his.'

No doubt any loyal member of Anne's household would dispute that. By sheer hard slog the Princess has overcome a lousy public image and won the respect of the entire country.

Less than three years after she hit the bottom of a royal popularity poll she was voted Woman of the Year. The critics who once rated her a royal pain in the posterior suddenly started hailing her as a selfless workaholic.

Even Fleet Street's most cynical hacks began to wonder what had happened to the haughty, horsey daughter of the Queen when they followed her around Africa on a Save the Children Fund tour in 1982. It was the most difficult and dangerous tour any royal lady had ever attempted. Anne set out to meet the charity workers in the field who do the dirtiest work of all. To get first-hand experience of what their lives are like she had to really rough it for the first time in her life.

'She had to sleep on camp beds like the rest of us,' explained one of the team who travelled with her. 'And she shared a bathroom with eight other people on certain sections of the trip.'

In three weeks the Princess covered 14,000 miles across six African countries. It was a gruelling journey into remote and disease-ridden areas where few people recognised their royal visitor. But this never bothered Anne.

'Quite possibly they didn't,' she admitted later. 'It didn't worry me. I didn't stop to ask if they knew who I was.'

The British press who dogged her every step of the way started out hoping to see a reunion between her and her husband Mark Phillips at a time when sizzling rumours were buzzing around Fleet Street that they were about to split.

The reunion did not take place on that trip, but Anne's ferocious hard work impressed them so much that the journalists ended up with a grudging respect for their quarry. Several members of the Press Pack decided to become sponsors of abandoned children in Kenya.

The tour became not just a personal triumph but a turning point. The public too began to notice that the Princess once renowned for her unbridled temper had turned into a royal workhorse. Princess Sourpuss had been transformed into a saintly woman thanks to some masterly work behind closed Palace doors. Chief instigator of the plan to salvage Anne's awful reputation was, it is believed, her father Prince Philip. His advice to his daughter was simple: work harder and all your troubles will fade away. But Anne's bloody-minded determination made the difference. A tough and resilient character like her father she has the guts to tackle almost any challenge.

She risked her regal neck as well as her pride when she became an Olympic and European champion in the eventing world and galloped down the Derby course to raise money for another favourite charity, Riding for the Disabled.

Princess Anne has always been spurred on by her resolve to be a person in her own right, not just the Queen's daughter, or Mtoto ya Queenie, the Swahili name they call her in Africa. She has always had before her the daunting image of Princess Margaret who never really found the right slot in the royal ranks or established herself as anything other than a glittering name in the gossip columns.

No royal social-security scrounger, Anne wants to be seen to be earning her hefty allowance from the Civil List. In 1987 the

Treasury gave her a £5,600 pay increase, bringing her annual income from the tax payers to £130,000. Most of this goes on staff salaries. Her husband Mark Phillips provides for his family by running their estate, Gatcombe Park in Gloucestershire, as a working farm. He also gets an income from lecturing and entering equestrian competitions all over the world.

Since Anne's first praiseworthy trek around Africa the Princess Royal has taken on even more commitments each year. She is one of the very few Royals who can be found out and about working over the Christmas and Easter holidays. She never seems to take a really long break.

At least she has found a satisfying role in life, but according to some unthinking royal observers her older brother Charles still seems to be searching for one.

Victor Chapman pours scorn on this idea. 'At times the Prince of Wales may complain that he does not seem to be achieving much, for instance for British trade when he tours overseas countries. But that is just because he tries to achieve too much too quickly. He only really got involved in promoting trade abroad about six years ago. He is keen to do a lot but it takes time to get results.'

Ever since the Prince of Wales left the Royal Navy in the late seventies people have been asking when he is going to get a 'proper job'.The general public has the idea that he needs one because he does not dedicate all his efforts to one single project the way most ordinary working men and women do.

It would be fairer to say that he has several jobs, like a director sitting on several different boards. But as everything he does is part-time the Queen's subjects get the idea that he only dabbles in the real workaday world.

On his passport his occupation is listed as Prince of Wales, a rather vague job description. He is by inclination a farmer when at home at Highgrove and through his involvement with the Duchy of Cornwall.

No doubt he could earn a reasonable living, if the monarchy was ever made redundant, by working as an author. He has written introductions for many books on such diverse subjects

51

as his grandmother, the Goons, anthropology and aircraft, as well as the very successful children's book, *The Old Man of Lochna'gar*, a story he dreamed up to entertain his younger brothers Andrew and Edward when they were small.

He might also make a very readable newspaper columnist. He has been an outspoken critic of modern architecture and caused a storm when he described a proposed extension for the National Gallery of Art in Trafalgar Square as 'a monstrous carbuncle on the face of an old friend'. And again when opening a £52 million micro-chip factory at Roborough, Devon, on the edge of Dartmoor, he made headlines by glaring at its bare metal and glass construction then declaring: 'I have heard the main hall described as an industrial cathedral. To me, it's more like a high-tech version of a Victorian prison.'

His grandmother, who probably understands the real Prince Charles better than almost anyone except his wife and his mother, feels she knows what sort of job would suit him best. The Queen Mother once declared: 'If there was anything left to discover in the world, Charles would have been an explorer.'

He has been called an ambassador and a diplomat for his sterling work flying the flag abroad. By forming the Prince's Trust, which raises money to help unemployed youngsters, and later the Prince's Charities Trust, he could quite reasonably call himself a social worker. About a third of his working hours are devoted to such good works, yet most of the nation have never heard of these charities or the benefits ordinary people gain from them.

Another favourite project is the United World Colleges. Before he sets off on overseas tours he gets briefings on any colleges in the areas he is to visit. If there are none the Prince tries to work into his schedule ways in which he could advance this cause with his host government.

Visiting a British Council office in Madrid in 1987 he broached the subject with some English language teachers. 'Have you heard of the United World Colleges?' he asked them. 'The United what?' replied one man, while all the others looked blank. 'Ah well, there's no point explaining now if you haven't heard about them,' said the Prince with a sigh. Such encounters remind him how much more work remains to be done.

The UWC was founded by Charles' much-loved great uncle Lord Mountbatten. He believed one excellent way to destroy prejudice and bring about racial harmony would be to educate students from different countries, cultural backgrounds and classes together. Today thousands of sixth formers are living and working closely in a series of colleges dotted around the globe all designed to increase world understanding.

Above all, Charles is an achiever: 'I'm one of those people who doesn't like sitting and watching someone else doing something,' he declares. He would always far rather be a participant than a spectator, which explains why he does not share his wife's excitement about the Wimbledon tournament each summer. He also gets none of the thrill his mother receives from watching one of her horses romp home first past the finishing post at Epsom or Ascot. 'I don't like going to the races to watch horses thundering up and down – I'd rather be riding one myself,' he explains.

It is a pity this drive is for the most part unrecognised by the British people who think he is merely filling in time until he finally reaches the throne.

5

Diana the Media Megastar

'Oh, you should have seen some of those Arabs going ga-ga when they saw me on the Gulf tour. I gave them the full treatment and they were just falling all over themselves. I just turned it on and mopped them up.'

The first thing you realise about the Princess of Wales once you get to know her even slightly is that she is an old-fashioned flirt. She 'turns it on', all the time, as she jokily boasted to reporters after her tour of Saudi Arabia.

She fixes a man with those teasing blue eyes and just smiles. She doesn't even have to open her mouth. That dynamite look says it all. And the message is unmistakable. 'I know I'm gorgeous. I know you think I'm gorgeous – but I'm spoken for.'

It is almost like a game she plays to beat the boredom of royal duties. 'I mop them up – just like that!' she says giggling. And you get the idea from her pleased grin that 'mopping them up' means knocking them dead in upper-class Sloane-speak.

But it's not just a bit of fun. It's Diana's way of reassuring herself that after six years she has still got them eating out of her hand. The proof is in the transfixed faces of the people she meets. No doubt about it, she is absolutely the greatest royal crowd-pleaser of all time.

A lot of her old chums clannishly refer to the Princess of Wales by her initials. POW. It's a sort of joke, okay? The

SuperSloane is definitely POW! personified. The world's most wanted Princess has proved that good background, good manners and a great marriage are what *really* matter. Keep out of the tacky gossip columns and you can wind up on the front page!

Diana Spencer was just a rich little nobody once. Now she has more fans than Madonna or Monroe. Long after they are forgotten she will be in all the history books. And she did it all without a single O-level or taking off her clothes, too!

It's wonderful to watch Diana, the mop-'em-up megastar, in action, switching on her high-voltage act in London's West End, Washington DC, Madrid and Melbourne as well as a lot of places in between. But she is at her billion kilowatt best when she gets all glammed up for a charity ball or some other glitzy engagement.

The performance begins when police motorcycle outriders screech to a halt outside the building, their sirens wailing a warning of her approach. A Rolls Royce purrs up behind them and pulls into the kerb. And as the crowds behind the barriers lining the street catch their first glimpse of her the ragged cheers die away to silent star-struck stares. The customised Rolls has specially enlarged windows so the people can see its royal occupant, and Diana sits up smiling in her motorised goldfish bowl.

Sliding out of the back seat she straightens up, turns, waves and then glides straight towards the open door ahead. An electronic storm of photographers' flashguns erupts on all sides as she disappears through the entrance.

Waiting inside are several hundred guests who may have paid megabucks to dine with her. The babble of conversation dies away as her Scotland Yard minder walks in clearing a path. And suddenly she is *there*. All the heads swivel, necks craning, eyes popping at the sight of the stunning Princess.

She sashays into the room, with head half lowered and looks up smiling from under her silky long lashes. Her expression is sexual dynamite – half cheeky, half childish. The effect is always the same – like a killer wave on a surfing beach she flattens everyone – it's a total wipeout. Every other woman in the place is outclassed, every man mesmerised.

The Princess knows it – and adores it. She is hooked on her own magnetic power. Those introduced get an even more dazzling impression close-up. Her complexion is flawlessly clear and lightly made-up. Only a faint blue liner around her eyes with perhaps a golden-beige sheen on her lids and a pale, peachy gloss on her lips. The whole effect is pearly, polished perfection.

Her face is not that of a great beauty. She has a largish nose and a small pointed chin. But the bone structure is good, and the features are well balanced so it is practically impossible to take a bad photograph of her. And then there is that knowing smile.

When she singles out a man for her special attention it takes a very cool character not to look totally thrown. Strong men go weak-kneed, sheiks go shaky, courtiers keel over and even presidents pale. And to Diana it's all a great giggle.

At a White House banquet in Washington DC superstars couldn't wait to cut in when President Reagan led her on to the ballroom floor in November 1985. While her husband did a majestic waltz with America's First Lady, Diana changed partners to boogie with John Travolta and Saturday night fever broke out all over the US capitol. A few minutes later Clint Eastwood whirled her away in his arms and later reported: 'She made my day!'

But the man she really wanted as her partner, Russian ballet star Mikhail Baryshnikov, had to sit entranced beside her all through dinner. He had injured a leg and was banned from the dance floor. All her life Diana has been mad about ballet and she is a great fan of the Bolshoi star who defected to live in America. So she showered him with sympathetic smiles and compliments, showing him she knew just what she was missing.

Diana revelled in the knowledge that men competed for her attention on other occasions too: in a desert camp an hour's drive from the Saudi Arabian capital, Riyadh, during a tour in

56

November 1986 she could have taught Scheherazade a few spellbinding lessons. Lounging against rich brocade cushions dressed in harem pants and blue silk tunic she sat cross-legged on a carpet.

In a scene straight out of the *Arabian Nights,* tribesmen in traditional robes wielding swords with solid gold handles whirled like dervishes in a wild dance. The Princess sat watching, saying little and sipping the thick black coffee offered to welcome all guests on arrival according to Middle Eastern custom. Peeping over the rim of her porcelain cup she smiled at an Arab prince.

Women are third-class citizens in the Arab world, born to serve men, and a wife is valued somewhere between a prize stallion and a racing camel. Diana changed all that in less time than it takes to say 'Allah be praised!'

When the royal party moved into another marquee where a sumptuous banquet was spread out, the dazzled prince decided to honour the slender blonde wife of Britain's future king by serving her himself. He ripped off a chunk of meat from a whole roast sheep with his bare hands and gave it to her. Diana smiled demurely and said: 'It's delicious.' But her eyes sparkled like the diamonds in her crescent moon earrings – a £10,000 gift from her Saudi hosts. She had done it again.

Her host in Saudi Arabia, the world's richest potentate King Fahd, astonished everyone by inviting the Princess to his palace. The only other female to have received this high honour was a woman astronaut whom he was obliged to have as his guest because she had rocketed into space with a Saudi prince in her crew.

It was the same story a few months later when she did her *femme fatale* act on the sixty-two-year-old President of Portugal, Dr Mario Soarez, in February 1987.

On a wintry night in Lisbon she arrived at the Ajuda Palace flaunting bare shoulders in a revealing strapless dress. Then she proceeded to give the President the works. She twanged his braces, fluttered her eyelashes and joked: 'If I get cold will you help warm me up?' She mopped him up in less than a minute.

It's significant that she goes into her amazing mopping-up routine more often when her husband is around. But her flirting seems just innocent fun. And no one ever takes advantage of her teasing or oversteps the mark between deference and disrespect. But it sometimes looks as if she is trying to remind Charles how desirable she is.

He publicly put her down once after a game of polo at Smith's Lawn, Windsor. A loud wolf whistle split the air as Diana walked out of the royal pavilion to present cups to the winning team. Prince Charles seemed a little annoyed, but he gave his wife a kiss to thank her for his prize. As if to get even she immediately wiped it off her lips with the back of her right hand.

Minutes later they began to slap and push one another in the car park. The battle Royal began when Diana gave Fergie's dad Major Ronald Ferguson a warm goodbye kiss and Prince Charles playfully hit her on the head saying: 'That's enough!'

Diana was not about to let him get away with that and kicked out at her laughing husband then gave him a hefty push. In return he shoved her back against her car. Diana then ducked for cover but as she jumped into the driving seat he brought one hand down in a karate chop on the back of her neck. Realising that people were staring in amazement the couple laughed, but no one was in much doubt that the pushing and shoving looked a little too forceful to be really funny.

Diana had always been a one-woman event right from the night of her first big formal engagement with her Prince in March 1981 when she wore that show-stopping black dress. But the big switch from demure Di to alluring lady occurred on Saturday 16 April 1983 when she attended a gala ball at the Hilton Hotel in Melbourne, Australia.

Her appearance that night was an unforgettable happening for everyone who witnessed it. Until then Diana had floated through formal evening engagements in swirling, full-skirted fairytale ballgowns. She had always looked as deliciously

The first press photo: Lady Diana Spencer, watching her Prince play polo at Midhurst, Sussex, August 1980

*Dodging the long lenses of cameramen at Balmoral, September 1980, Diana
proved she was no easy catch*

On a trek into the Himalayas Prince Charles was just a whisker away from asking Diana to be his bride

A wide-eyed Di on her way to a Royal Academy reception with Charles shortly before their wedding

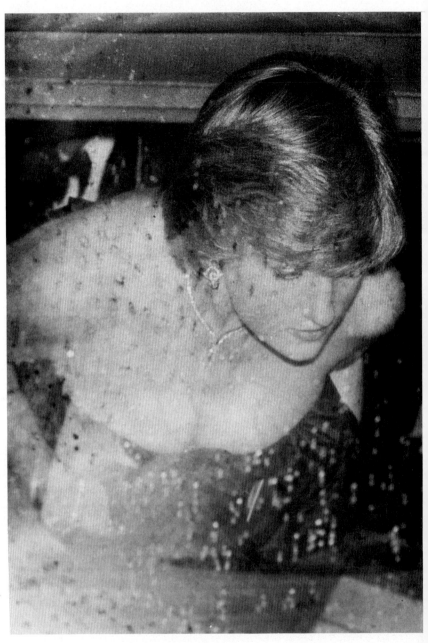

Diana's breathtaking black evening gown stunned royal watchers at the Goldsmith's Hall, London, in March 1981

The train now standing at St Paul's is 21 feet long

Above: proud papa Charles takes William, his firstborn, home from hospital in June 1982

Left: breaking a royal rule: two heirs to the throne, Charles and his son William, fly together to Scotland

Diana's darling: Prince Harry on holiday with his mother in Majorca

A majestic waltz in Melbourne, Australia 1985

romantic as if she had stepped straight out of a Winterhalter portrait on the walls of Windsor Castle.

But right at the end of her tour Down Under Diana tossed away those demure, girlish gowns and proved she was a sophisticated lady. She wore a white figure-hugging, crepe de Chine silk dress that clung to every curve and shimmered with crystal embroidery as she moved. Its slinky design bared one beautifully tanned shoulder and moulded itself to her body like a glittering second skin. It was a movie star marvel of a dress that only a very self-assured woman could wear. And Diana knew the electric effect it had on her audience.

She was making a declaration that a new Di had dawned. She had moved out of the ranks of coy royal wives into superstar status. And she wanted the world to know it.

Her first royal tour overseas had been a sell-out success. Record crowds had cheered her from Alice Springs to Adelaide, from Brisbane to Bendigo. She had faced the worst that the drought, flood and fire ravaged country could throw at her. After that gruelling six-week slog around Australia and New Zealand the royal novice had become a pro. From now on she wasn't going to be just a pretty, expensive supporting act for her husband, but the main event.

One night I stood at the door as she walked into another ballroom at the Sheraton-Wentworth Hotel in Sydney. The explosion of flashguns in my face as she entered blinded me for fully five minutes. I couldn't see anything until my eyes recovered from the electronic onslaught. But Diana swanned past me, head up, smiling through the blitz as if the hordes of cameramen were not even there. A thousand eyes were on her. They were checking her make-up, valuing her jewellery, taking her flounced, blue evening dress apart at the seams. Her poise, her posture, and her glossy hair all got non-stop scrutiny all night, even her hands were examined for signs of nervous nail-biting.

Everyone had wondered what the future queen was really like. And they were prepared to pay well for tickets to find out. She did not disappoint them.

After six years Diana still loves the adulation. No woman on earth can equal her unique blend of status and sex appeal. Other women may be more beautiful, more wealthy or more powerful. But no one, not even the Queen, is so glamorous and so gloriously royal. Very few women are ever placed on such a pedestal. Maybe only one or two each century would come close. Other women live and die and are remembered only by their families for a generation or two. But a Queen of England, which she will one day be, will be remembered as long as history is written. It must be a heady feeling.

Despite the down side – the loss of privacy, the protocol and pomp – Diana still seems to enjoy her job. Even when a job is tedious or taxing she seems buoyed up by the waves of warmth from the crowds who always surround her.

But such astounding success may create tension in a happy marriage. Almost from the first time she went anywhere with her husband she upstaged him. From the first day of their first tour together the Prince was overshadowed by his gorgeous young wife. At first Prince Charles didn't mind too much. When crowds in Wales pointedly ignored him just three months after their marriage and called for Diana he joked: 'I'm sorry, I've only got one wife and she's over there on the other side of the street. You'll have to make do with me instead.'

But gradually the Princess's popularity became embarrassing. It was especially noticeable on walkabouts when cameramen clustered around her while totally neglecting her husband. At times the far more important Prince was so overlooked that royal aides would plead with the press: 'For God's sake, can't one of you stick with him? It looks so awful if you all cover the Princess.'

Prince Charles' natural feeling of resentment gradually became more obvious. When a cheeky little boy about ten years old saw him at Silverstone race track and yelled: 'Oi, Charlie, where's Di?' he did not look at all amused. 'She's not here, there's only me, so you'd better go and ask for your money back,' he said somewhat bitterly.

Whenever they went anywhere together her smiling photograph made all the papers next day but he was usually cut out of the picture. To try to prevent this Diana began ducking her head when cameramen were around so that they would get unusable shots of her.

But the press misunderstood. They thought she was being moody, and accused her of being a prima donna princess. Eventually she gave up the struggle to stay in the background, which she did not enjoy much anyway, she had a much bigger problem to tackle.

The sensational designer clothes everyone admired were her only interest, the press reported. The Princess was a hopeless shopaholic never happier than when cruising through Harrods or Harvey Nichols and visiting the top designer salons scattered around the Knightsbridge area, they claimed.

Palace advisers became concerned that the public was only aware of what Diana wore on public duties, not what she was actually doing. But usually the way she looked was much more fascinating than any job she did. After the birth of Prince Harry she posed for a family portrait with her children. Lord Snowdon was the photographer and he used a stylist and make-up artist to produce a new Diana with heavy make-up and a sultry expression.

The pictures from this session launched the era of 'Dynasty Di', the Princess with more pizzazz than any Hollywood soap star. When Britain's Queen of Fashion met Joan Collins, the Queen of Hollywood, Diana proved she could out-dazzle any superstar in showbiz. But Palace advisers began worrying that her glitzy image might trivialise the monarchy.

Speculation about her spending sprees reached ridiculous heights when a small circulation newspaper desperate for a sensational story claimed that Diana had spent £100,000 on a new wardrobe for a tour of Italy in 1985.

Fed up with the fuss about her clothes Diana surprised everyone by wearing one old outfit after another. Photographers, accustomed to seeing her in a fantastic new fashion every day, groaned when she arrived at the opera in Milan wearing a pale pink organza gown first seen in Australia two years earlier.

The *Sun* newspaper's royal photographer Arthur Edwards decided to tackle her about this disappointing dress. A genuine East Ender unimpressed by rank or riches, he believes the Royal Family are surrounded by yes-men and occasionally enjoy a conversation with someone who treats them like a human being not a holy cow.

The Princess of Wales for one will always make sure he gets a good picture of her by looking straight into his lens. He is the only Fleet Street photographer she addresses by his christian name. 'I really love him. He makes me laugh. He's somehow different from all the others,' she told a group of us in Spain while our Arfur had the grace to blush.

So when the Princess greeted him cheerily the morning after her night at the opera Arthur 'steamed in' to her, as he would put it. 'Why did you have to wear that old boring dress?' he bluntly asked.

Diana laughed. 'Oh, I suppose you'd like it better if I came naked,' she teased.

'Well, at least then I'd get a picture of ya in the paper,' said Arthur refusing to be won over by her charm.

But on that visit to Italy Diana wore so many old outfits the press dubbed her 'Second Hand Rosa' and began asking if Britain's Queen of Fashion was 'Pasta her Besta'.

The Princess didn't care. She had drawn up a plan to kill off Diana the Darling of the Dress Designers and introduce the world to a hard-working young mum. She was tired of being seen as nothing more than an adorable dumb belle. Her wardrobe and weight-watching filled endless pages with mind-blowing trivia in women's magazines, which made Prince Charles grumble about 'the unutterable rubbish ... written about my wife from time to time'.

People often mentioned that, given her educational record, it wasn't so surprising that babies and boutiques were all she cared about. They pointed out that she is a TV soap opera addict, likes London's rock radio station Capital switched on whenever she is at home, and was once caught giggling during 'God Save the Queen'. Obviously, she is the lady least likely to win 'Mastermind', some reckon.

Diana has helped to perpetuate such ideas by apparently putting herself down in public. On a visit to a Dr Barnardo's home in Hull she met a sixteen-year-old boy who was telling her he was worried about passing the exams he needed to get a job. Diana tried to cure his anxiety. She confessed: 'I never got any O-levels – always too busy. Brain the size of a pea, I've got.'

Again, at an old folks' home near Newcastle-upon-Tyne she confessed she was useless at playing cards. 'I like playing bridge, but I'm no good – I talk too much,' she told pensioner Robina Reynolds.

These comments were just jokey ways of putting nervous members of the public at their ease, a kind gesture from a caring woman. But they have lingered in the public's mind. And TV shows like 'Spitting Image', which portray her as an empty-headed Sloane Ranger nattering non-stop about pop stars, have made the dense label stick.

The real Diana, however, is a very different person. Far from being bored by her husband's mature and learned friends she now really enjoys their company. Charles' closest adviser Sir Laurens van der Post has particularly impressed her. 'Listening to him talk is so wonderful,' she says. 'It is like meeting a god. He is such a fascinating man.'

The exposure to people from all walks of life – the talented, the terminally ill, the disabled and the disadvantaged – has made her a more thoughtful, mature person. Endless hours of briefings from royal aides have also helped. She can now talk knowledgeably on a wide range of topics and hold her own with heads of state and celebrities.

One of Prince Charles' staff summed up the real situation: 'Do you really think he would want to saddle himself with a wife who was just a gorgeous idiot? He has met too many in his time to want to spend the rest of his days with one.'

Reporters and photographers know a quick-witted woman who can shoot them down with a funny one-liner in any encounter. But these conversations rarely get reported because they are usually just chit-chat and not newsy enough to publish.

Diana has always resented her reputation as a dunce but mostly managed to keep it hidden. Her simmering annoyance boiled over one day in Italy in 1985. As she trailed around the architectural glories of Florence behind her husband, toffee-nosed dignitaries made it plain they thought she was no culture vulture. 'The Princess did ask some questions but it was obviously all new to her,' was one patronising comment after the couple had been shown around Florence cathedral.

Then one morning as they walked through a low arch in a garden Prince Charles warned his lofty lady: 'Mind your head!' Diana replied: 'Why? There's nothing in it.' Her bitter crack was loud enough to be overheard by the accompanying officials.

The time had come to destroy the myth of the feather-brained fashion plate. She began slowly to make more speeches in public. She also got involved with some serious projects. Joining the war against drug abuse she signed a public pledge as part of Westminster Council's Say No campaign. Her signature was soon joined by those of Rolling Stone Bill Wyman, Cliff Richard and Dire Straits' John Illsley.

Her equerry Lieutenant Commander Richard Aylard later revealed: 'The Princess made a special study of the heroin problem in Britain. She is one of the best-informed people on it now. She once surprised a top drugs expert when she met him by saying: "Oh yes, I know all about you. I've read your book on heroin."'

But shaking off her old, unflattering image may take a very long time. When the Princess toured the Prado Museum in Madrid in April 1987 an official who acted as her guide admitted she had not expected that Diana would appreciate its treasures. 'The Princess knew which paintings were by whom. She recognised every Velázquez and Goya before I could say a word,' said the surprised deputy director of the museum.

Today the Princess is a real swot. Before every trip abroad she does extensive research on the places she will go to and the people she will meet. Richard Aylard adds: 'She certainly does her homework. She does a lot of research and works hard to do her job well. I write all her briefings and I certainly don't write down to her. The reason she is stuck with this unfair image is she did not have a very academic education. But that doesn't mean she isn't intelligent. Quite the reverse, in fact.'

Now patron or president of more than twenty charities the Princess takes an active interest in each. Although she would reject any suggestion that she favours any one of them, she seems to have singled out Dr Barnardo's Homes for her fullest support and certainly impressed its spokesman, Bill Beaver, with her dedication.

'Since the Princess became our president we have been floored by her quick brain,' he revealed. 'The trouble is she has this gooey image and people expect to see something sweet that has just stepped out of a chocolate box. But when you see her in action you get a surprise. She is not just a figurehead president. She has this astonishing concentration of mind and cuts straight to the heart of a problem. Top industrialists come to see us and don't show the same high level understanding of our problems.

'The Princess definitely keeps us on our toes. Her questions are so incisive. She hears some horrific stories and meets some kids that have been in Borstals or come very close to it. I don't know any other woman her age, except maybe a social worker, who has such a terrific grasp of the Social Services. And she stuns some people when she knows their backgrounds and remembers their names.'

Diana now spends long hours at her desk reading reports on all the organisations she heads. And everywhere she goes she takes a briefcase packed with paperwork.

To assist in her work for the British Deaf Association she decided to learn sign language. The BDA General Secretary Bernard Quinn explained: 'We sent her a video on how to learn to communicate and after daily half-hour sessions for two weeks she mastered it. But what impressed us was not that she got it right but that she had the nerve to try her new skill out in front of a crowd of people. She could have made mistakes and looked very foolish.'

Worried about the needless suffering caused when mothers get rubella (or German measles as it is better known) during the early stages of pregnancy she asked what she could do to warn young girls they should be vaccinated. Finally, she decided to write a letter which the National Rubella Association could use in the fight to prevent babies being born deaf, blind and mentally handicapped.

Her letter has been endlessly copied and circulated through out the country so that its message may reach every family, school and women's organisation. 'It is not enough to think that you have had rubella in the past,' Diana warned. 'The disease is difficult to confirm without a blood test. So the best safety is in the vaccine.'

But while the Princess steadily increased her workload her husband began cutting back on public engagements. At first, it was believed that he was determined to spend as much time as possible with his children while they were small, aware that once he became king he would have far fewer hours for his family.

But gradually it became more obvious that the Prince was spending his increased leisure time away from his wife and sons. When the Wales family did get together for holidays Charles frequently spent hours on his own just strolling around the Sandringham estate or fishing in the River Dee at Balmoral.

Diana naturally resented being left alone so often. She told friends that she thought her husband was being selfish. But one man who knows the couple well commented: 'I don't think the Prince is aware that his wife feels neglected. Most of the time he seems to be off in some world of his own where she can't reach him.'

When he goes off on tour without his wife he seems like a different man. He is once again the centre of attention and looks much happier. On his spring 1987 visit to southern Africa he seemed very relaxed, cracking jokes and going out of his way to pose for pictures. When presented with a souvenir warrior's shield and an arrow-headed spear by King Mswati III in Swaziland, the Prince replied that he appreciated the gifts 'which I will try very hard to prevent my children getting hold of – they might do me some extreme damage'. In Malawi he told a story from his bachelor days to a group of scholars who had studied in London. He reckoned that they probably knew the place better than he did. 'I am one of those hopeless people who can never find their way around because the streets keep changing to one way,' he explained. 'One night I wanted to drive in my car without my policeman who usually comes with me, because I wanted to go and visit a girlfriend in another part of London. So I said: "You lead me in your car and I'll follow." Well, my police officer had a red Mini. And suddenly when we reached Marble Arch ten red Minis appeared and I ended up half-way down Oxford Street miles from where I was supposed to be. Eventually, by good luck rather than good management I found my way to the right street where I met my policeman, totally unconcerned, waiting for me to turn up.'

As he finished telling this little tale against himself one of his aides leaned over and whispered: 'He wouldn't have mentioned that story if the Princess had been here.'

Victor Chapman explained what he thought were the reasons for the Prince's good mood throughout his tour: 'When he gets out on his own he does his thing. He sees all the photographers aiming at him and he gives them something special.' Three weeks later on a tour of Spain with Princess Diana the Prince had once again to put up with his wife stealing the show every day. He did not exchange quips with reporters during working hours or create fun pictures for friendly photographers. Life was back to normal.

During a sightseeing tour of Salamanca, an ancient university town with some of the most glorious architecture in Spain, the Princess suddenly seemed unwell.

After an official welcome from the mayor in the main square the royal couple set off on a walking tour of the town. The temperature was in the high eighties and the crowded streets

67

were hot and dusty. As she entered Salamanca university Diana sank down on a medieval wooden bench and rested her head on her arms. A few minutes later in the library she turned pale and shaky, and emerged clutching her head in her hands.

While touring a museum she walked away from the royal party to stand against a wall as if too tired to continue. It was a hot day and she had been on her feet for almost three hours without a break. Prince Charles hurried over to ask if she was all right. She nodded and rejoined the museum tour. But a few minutes later her lady-in-waiting Anne Beckwith-Smith asked for some aspirin to be fetched from the royal car.

The journalists who had been following the royal party were puzzled. Only minutes earlier Diana had seemed perfectly well. Was she really ill? Or was she just bored with an overdose of culture? Before they could decide, the pressmen and women were asked to leave the building while Diana went into a private room to rest for ten minutes. After a drink and a visit to the powder room she reappeared looking much better. The British Ambassador's wife Lady Gordon-Lennox, who was with the Princess when she freshened up, said as the tour proceeded: 'I think the heat and the crowds just proved a bit too much. You know, you need a lot of stamina and a strong bladder to be royal.'

Later tour officials played down the incident claiming that the Princess was perfectly well. But her fainting spell on a visit to Canada in 1986 raised questions about Diana's health once again.

The Queen has never once come close to keeling over in public although she has frequently carried on working while far from well. She always manages to hide any discomfort in case she disappoints people. Princess Anne is another tough trouper who gamely gets up and walks away from serious falls from her horses. She also impressed journalists tremendously once on a tour of Ethiopia by keeping a stiff upper lip right through a banquet when suffering a bad case of rumbling tum. Only at the very last second did she allow herself to dash out with one hand over her mouth. Princess Margaret, whom no one would imagine was the Spartan sort, has attended charity balls almost prostrate from the pain of a migraine. Smiling through gritted teeth is a golden rule with royal ladies.

Diana at first seemed no different. On a visit to Chesterfield in the early months of her first pregnancy she looked pale and on the point of collapse. But despite her morning sickness the Princess insisted on carrying out a long day of official duties.

Since then she has gained a more relaxed attitude to her job. Diana does things her way. And if she wilts in the heat or feels faint then she is only human just like the rest of us. And if she is a bit fed up at times that may be a tiny bit obvious too.

But she was upset when some journalists criticised her for giggling during a passing out parade at Sandhurst where she represented the Queen. The Princess felt it was unfair to claim she was not doing the job with dignity.

'First of all, standing in for the Queen made me incredibly nervous and when I'm nervous I tend to giggle,' she explained. 'But while I was trying hard to look composed the commandant at Sandhurst kept telling me jokes the whole time. They weren't great jokes. In fact, they were pretty feeble. But I had to laugh just to be polite. But I didn't think they should criticise me when I was doing my best.'

Rather appropriately for a passing out parade Diana had worn an outfit which has been called her chocolate soldier outfit. A slinky white military style coatdress decorated with gold frogging, it looked like she had rented it from a fancy dress hire company.

She had worn it first when greeting King Fahd of Saudi Arabia on his official visit to Britain in 1987. The world's richest man was totally upstaged by the woman who welcomed him at Gatwick airport. The next day all the newspapers featured pictures of Diana and filled more columns reporting what she wore than who she met.

It was proof once again that Diana the media megastar can always knock anyone off the front page – even the world's richest king.

If there was any doubt that she revels in publicity it was

banished in the autumn of 1986 when Di was on holiday at Balmoral with her family. One morning she went out for a walk holding four-year-old Prince William by the hand. Dressed casually in jeans and jumper she took her son for a stroll through the grounds of the castle. 'Are there any journalists around today?' she asked a policeman who passed her on patrol. 'Yes, Ma'am, there are several down on the riverbank opposite. I would advise you to keep well away from the area,' he warned.

Diana thanked the officer and walked off through the shrubbery. But instead of heeding his advice she headed straight for the south bank of the River Dee. A few minutes later the photographers who had been scanning the water's edge all morning from a concealed viewpoint were rewarded when the Princess and William, apparently unaware of their presence, skipped down through the trees to the water's edge.

Squinting through their 600 millimetre lenses they watched mother and son messing about on the muddy shore. First, Diana picked up some pebbles, urging William to do the same. Then she taught him the correct way to throw them so they would skip across the calm surface of the river. One by one small stones skittered across the water then landed plop! further out in the deep mainstream.

When they tired of this game she began tickling him and tossing him high in the air. Enjoying the fun, William squealed and tried to wriggle out of her grasp as his mother held him upside down and pretended that she was going to throw him into the cold water. Then as soon as she gave in and put him down he begged her to do it all over again.

As their motordrives whirred and shutters clicked the cameramen could not believe their luck. They had a set of pictures that were guaranteed to get a big spread in the newspapers next day. Not one of them realised then that the Princess knew very well that they were hidden on the other side of the river. The future Queen of England had decided to stage a show especially for them.

6

Heirs and Graces

As Princess Diana dropped her son William with his royal body-guard at school one morning a woman approached her in the hallway. 'My son is in the same class as yours,' she said. 'Last night when my husband came home our son told his father that there was a very lucky boy at his school called William.'

The Princess bit her lip as if wondering whether her son's schoolfriends had twigged how very different her four-year-old son was from the rest of them.

But the woman smiled and went on: 'My son said that this William was lucky because his father came to school with him every morning and stayed with him all day. He wanted to know why his dad couldn't come to classes with him the way William's did.'

Diana rocked with laughter, relieved that for the moment the real reason why William had a Scotland Yard shadow at school had not leaked out to his curious friends.

Prince Charles and his wife agreed a secret pact when both their sons were babies that for as long as possible they would not be told that they are in any way special or more important than their friends. No one in the Royal Household mentions William's title or the glittering future lying before him. He is 'just William' to all the staff at home and at school, by royal command.

Charles once explained rather movingly how it feels to learn that you are not an ordinary little boy, but heir to the throne.

'I think it's something that dawns on you with the most ghastly, inexorable sense,' he declared. 'I didn't suddenly wake up in my pram one day and say "Yippee" ... slowly you get the idea that you have a certain duty and responsibility, and I think it's better that way, rather than somebody suddenly telling you.'

He certainly hopes that no little know-all at school will drop the news on William like a nuclear missile. To date both Charles and Diana have explained away the attention directed at their son with a few harmless fibs.

'When William asked me why there were so many men with cameras in the street outside his nursery I told him the photographers weren't there to take his picture,' the Princess once confessed. 'I said to William: "They just want to take pictures of me in my new dress, that's all." And he seemed satisfied with that. But the next day there were no photographers at all, and he couldn't understand it. He thought they waited there every day.'

Prince Charles is very much aware that when he is finally crowned king he could be in his late fifties or even older. His mother is more healthy and active than most women in their sixties and may continue to reign for twenty or even thirty years.

This means that Charles III may be monarch for a relatively short time, while William could take over after his death and rule for more than half the twenty-first century. He must therefore be trained for a life of service to his kingdom and the Commonwealth.

But as William approached school age his father became concerned that his son and heir was becoming a little monster. Wilful William ran riot around his home and, so it seemed to his father, he was fast becoming a precocious, pampered little prince.

He almost destroyed the Queen Mother's dining room at Birkhall once when his parents took him there for lunch. At the time he was only two years old and his mother was already declaring publicly that her son behaved like a 'mini-tornado'.

William also caused a security alert at Balmoral when he pressed a button on the wall of the nursery setting off the alarm system and bringing squads of police and Special Branch detectives rushing to the castle from all over Aberdeenshire. William, or Wombat as his father calls him after the animal in an Australian storybook, was growing up as wild as any creature in the outback Down Under.

Worst of all, the whole world seemed to know it. Millions of television viewers saw the Queen upstaged by her grandson at the christening of Prince Harry. Paying no heed to the distinguished, elderly assembly of royals, politicians and churchmen (including the Archbishop of Canterbury), William ran unchecked through the Palace, butting old ladies and shrieking with glee.

The Queen attempted to stop the little terror by grabbing his arm as he rushed past her. 'What's the name of my new puppy, William?' she asked. 'It's a word that comes out frightfully well when we're cross. You know, it's Dash, isn't it? We say, Oh, Dash!' But the only dash William was interested in was right across the room. He wriggled out of her grasp and ran off chasing his little cousin Zara, Princess Anne's daughter.

Pictures of four-year-old William poking his tongue out in photographs taken on the Duke and Duchess of York's wedding day were splashed across the front pages of newspapers around the globe. Gossip columns were full of his pranks, occasionally exaggerated or untrue, but always embarrassing.

At his nursery school in Notting Hill the parents of other children nicknamed him 'Billy the Basher' because he started so many playground battles. And when his parents turned up to see their little treasure performing as a wolf in the nursery's Christmas play he burst into tears when he spotted them from the stage. Only when a teacher quickly produced a packet of sweets could the sobbing little actor be persuaded that the show had to go on.

Soon after his fourth birthday in 1986 Prince Charles decided it was time to introduce his son to the great passion of his life –

polo. But William had to be whisked away from Smith's Lawn in Windsor Great Park because he exhausted his mother by climbing up the edge of the royal box and chattering non-stop. Diana repeatedly pulled her son back to safety by the seat of his royal blue pants but finally gave up and took him home.

'But it was not so much what William did as what he said that upset his father,' explains one member of the Prince's staff. 'Almost from the time he could talk he was a cheeky little sod. He used to speak to grown-ups as if they were stupid, although he was such a cutie none of us ever cared. He definitely has his mother's wicked charm whereas his little brother Harry is a very quiet kid.'

The answer to this problem seemed to be someone with a firm hand. But royal nanny Barbara Barnes, who had cared for the little prince and his brother from birth, had always idolised William. 'She loved him so much she let him get away with murder,' says the man from the Palace. 'The trouble was she did not seem to give quite as much affection to little Harry. William ran around creating havoc in the Royal Household.'

Many other members of Charles and Diana's staff became convinced that William was becoming a precocious little snob.

In December 1986 Barbara had been a guest along with Princess Margaret, movie star Raquel Welch and 200 other celebrities at the lavish sixtieth birthday party of her previous employer Lord Glenconner. The former Colin Tennant had invited her not as a servant, but as a family friend to fly out to his holiday home on the ritzy resort Mustique. 'People were greeting the royal nanny in exactly the same way they were greeting Princess Margaret,' said another guest. 'She was perfectly at ease as if among equals.'

Barbara grew up on the estate of the Earl of Leicester, Lady Glenconner's father, where her father was employed as a forestry worker until his retirement. She had no formal training when she began working for Princess Margaret's closest friends, the Glenconners, in 1967. And when their youngest children, twins Amy and May Tennant, went to boarding school at eleven the Princess recommended her to Charles and Diana.

Barbara joined them in 1982 when Prince William was born.

As Nanny Barnes revelled in the party scene on Mustique it seemed to some that she had outgrown her nanny's job. And back at Kensington Palace, the other staff were quick to notice. 'She became quite grand, almost as if she was royal herself,' explains another Palace worker. 'For example, she used to ask the footmen to clean the children's shoes instead of doing it herself. They were fetching and carrying for her all the time. William started to get the idea that the Palace employees were just lackeys to be ordered about.

'Barbara used to love going up to Sandringham at New Year because a special footman was attached to the nursery there. And she was given the use of her own chauffeur. That was very handy because she comes from Norfolk and was allowed to whizz off in a royal car to visit her family who live some miles away.'

When she travelled with the children to Highgrove it was often a different story. One of the domestic staff revealed: 'Poor little Harry sometimes arrived from London by car in a terrible state. He cried all the way down from Kensington Palace because he got so car sick. Of course, Barbara did her best to mop him up and opened the car window to give him fresh air. She was obsessed with William. Harry was always well-scrubbed, dressed and brushed but the older boy always seemed to get more of her affection.'

Prince Charles became concerned that his son was not learning to respect other people. 'The Prince treats everyone on his staff as if they were as well-born as he is,' explains the Kensington Palace worker.

'He never orders anyone to do anything. He always asks. For instance, he has politely asked everyone on his staff, "Would you mind if my children called you by your christian name?" He doesn't want them to think they are anything special or any better than anyone else.'

Despite his love for his son Prince Charles was sensible enough to realise that if Wild Willie Wales continued to be such a handful he could grow into a spoiled, arrogant prig of prince. He would then undoubtedly become a disastrous king.

His late great uncle Lord Mountbatten used to say that the monarchy would last only as long as kings and queens were worthy of the job. A cousin of the Russian Czar, Britain's King and Germany's Kaiser, Uncle Dickie, as the Queen's family called him, grew up with the twentieth century and gradually watched many of his royal relatives lose their thrones through stupidity, pride or bad luck.

When he wondered why the British throne remained so stable he concluded it was because his English cousins were not glamorous figureheads but hard-working and modest. He also saw these admirable qualities embodied in his great-nephew Prince Charles.

But the next monarch King Charles would have to make certain that his heirs also remembered his Uncle Dickie's words of warning.

This idea was obviously on Prince Charles' mind when he considered the best way to raise a little boy who will come of age in the year 2000 and reign over a society changing at an even more rapid rate than ours is today.

He was concerned because his wife had a far more relaxed attitude to child care. Diana's experience as an assistant at the Young England kindergarten in London persuaded her that all lively children are naughty from time to time, and she often smiled indulgently at William's antics.

Many couples clash when it comes to raising good citizens of the future. But for Diana and Charles the problem of William was far more serious. No one would envy these parents as they select for their sons an education that will make them worthy of the throne.

Under their guidance William must follow not his own interests, but tutoring, grooming and grounding in subjects that will satisfy the demands of his high position. He must be smart but not a know-all, well informed but never patronising. He must have sound opinions but never force them on other people. He must be dedicated and hard-working but never seem harassed or overwhelmed by his job. And if all this sounds as if he must be superhuman, that is the very last thing he should appear.

While Charles worried what was the best way to approach the task of raising a future king, Diana was more relaxed. 'I always feel he will be all right because he has been born to his royal role. He will get accustomed to it gradually,' she once explained to a group of reporters. Her husband was not so sure.

Soon their opposing attitudes to their son's upbringing created a series of disagreements that upset both of them. In her view it was vitally important that William should have as normal a childhood as possible. Her husband, with the benefit of his own experience, wondered if a boy born to be king can ever really be normal. If William had to lose what every other child enjoyed – an ordinary, carefree childhood – that was unfortunately a price that must be paid. Diana, however, disagreed. William would be hampered by royal rules and obligations soon enough, she argued. Trying to control his natural impish nature would simply not work, and remembering her own childish escapades she declared: 'He'll grow out of it.'

When tackled by reporters once for a comment on the royal rascal's latest prank Diana grinned and said: 'William is just like me – always in trouble.'

Staff at Sandringham were amazed when she calmly watched William misbehave and refused to do anything about it. In January 1987 the entire Royal Household took part in a fire drill and young William rushed out on to the lawn with his mother to watch the shiny red fire engines draw up in front of the house.

He started chatting to the firemen and climbed up on to the rear platform of one engine to see how its equipment worked. One friendly young fire fighter asked William if he would like to try on his helmet.

'Oh yes, please,' said the excited little prince. Then he ran around in circles showing off his new prize.

When the drill finished and everyone began filing back into the house Diana told her son to return the helmet. 'No, it's mine. I'm keeping it,' William said defiantly.

'Be a good boy, the fireman needs it,' the Princess protested. 'No, I want it. I want it!' he screamed. Then ignoring her pleas to come back William ran off around the corner of the house and disappeared from sight.

Diana simply shrugged her shoulders and giggled. 'I'm sorry,' she said to the embarrassed owner of the helmet. 'When he puts it down we'll find it and have it sent back to you.'

A BBC television film crew also were surprised when Princess Diana bribed her son to perform for their cameras by promising him a sweet biscuit.

Wayward William was taking part in a BBC documentary about the Duchy of Cornwall. But when asked to walk across a field with his father he shook his head and ran away. Repeated requests to return did not work. So Diana tried an old trick. Tea and biscuits had been produced for the film crew. Pointing out a dish of shortbread the Princess said to her son: 'Darling, you can have a biscuit afterwards if you're a good boy.' William immediately took his father's hand and said: 'Come on, Papa.'

Reporter Jenni Murray, who interviewed Prince Charles for the film, said later: 'It was important to have William in the film because he will become Duke of Cornwall when his father is king. The bribery was worthwhile because I think the best scene we shot was of the Prince taking William around the farm at Highgrove explaining to him the different breeds of sheep they have there.'

Jenni asked Prince Charles if he had any advice to pass on to his son. 'If a son pays any attention to advice proffered by a father,' Charles hedged. 'I didn't listen to advice from my own father until I was in my late teens. I hadn't paid any attention before.'

He added that he hoped William would learn a lot just by hanging around with his dad 'rather like a farmer's son by following his father around the farm picking things up, he will do the same'. But the best advice of all he could give William as the next Duke of Cornwall, said the Prince, is 'to make sure he has got advisers around him, to choose the right people to help him do the job'.

Although a devoted dad who willingly changed nappies and even jumped into the bath tub with his sons, Charles has always tried to be consistently firm when necessary. He believes in traditional styles of parenting and is particularly keen that his children should learn self-discipline.

An example of his no-nonsense methods happened at Balmoral when he decided to give William a riding lesson. At the time his number one son was very fond of the Queen's groom Doreen Cashman and began crying for her when his father lifted him astride his Shetland pony Smokey.

'No, no! I want Doreen,' William yelled and big crocodile tears ran down his little face. Charles took absolutely no notice. Despite screams of protest he led the pony around the stable yard until William realised he was not going to get his own way.

As the Prince could not always be around to see that his son was made to behave he decided some extra help was needed. It was obvious that William needed far more discipline. And if Nanny Barnes could not find it in her heart to take a tough line with his little tearaway then perhaps someone else would.

The Prince and his wife decided privately that they did not want any more disruptions in their household. Too many members of their staff had been given the Royal Order of the Boot, so gossips claimed. Each time another royal employee resigned or was fired, reports appeared in the press that Diana was to blame.

To avoid another storm of stories about 'Malice in the palace' they simply decided to make it clear that things weren't working out with Barbara. 'Nanny Barnes got the message all right,' the man from the Palace adds. 'The Princess is always incredibly friendly to everyone. But suddenly she stopped being so nice to Barbara. The message finally filtered through and Barbara handed in her notice.'

On 15 January 1987, the day Prince William started lessons at Wetherby School, Buckingham Palace issued a surprise announcement. Barbara Barnes, the royal nanny for almost five years, was leaving, it revealed. A Palace spokesman explained: 'As Prince William is now to attend school full-time it has been mutually decided by Miss Barnes and the Prince and Princess that it is an appropriate time for her to move.'

As royal nannies normally stay with their charges until they are at least eleven or twelve years old most Palace observers felt her departure was a shock and decided that it was the result of behind-the-scenes pressure. They were convinced when Anne, Lady Glenconner later revealed that Prince Charles was the main reason Barbara decided to sever her ties with the Royal Household. After a holiday in the West Country Nanny Barnes went back to caring for other people's children as a temp.

She was quickly replaced by Ruth Wallace, described by friends as a 'brisk and businesslike' woman. Until she took on the job of caring for the little princes Ruth, a forty-year-old nurse, had devoted her life to sick children. After qualifying she decided to work in the children's casualty and radio-therapy unit at St Bartholomew's hospital in the City of London.

But for six years before her royal appointment she had worked part time for the family of ex-King Constantine of Greece, a close friend of Charles and Diana.

Almost immediately after she joined the household the staff noticed a tremendous difference. 'William and Harry are changed children,' insists the Palace worker. 'William is far more polite to everyone and Harry hardly ever cries now. He seems a lot happier.

'Both the boys immediately seemed to take to "Roof", as they call her. She encourages them to be friendly and chat to all the staff. Barbara was not like that. She used to take the children to visit the stables at Sandringham or Balmoral to see the ponies. In her book that is quite an upper-class thing to do.

'I have seen the new nanny take the children to the garages where their own little electric cars are kept and they have hours of fun playing with them. That never happened in the past.'

Nanny Wallace spends less time with her charges now that both boys are at school. William and Harry are the first children so close to the throne to begin their education in an ordinary schoolroom. Both their parents started lessons at home with a governess. Aware that the little princes spend more time than most surrounded by adults Charles and Diana felt it important to give them a taste of the rough and tumble of real life as early as possible.

When he was three William became a pupil at Mrs Mynors' nursery school in Notting Hill, west London. His little brother follows him there in September 1987 just before his third birthday. Jane Mynors runs one of London's smartest private kindergartens in the basement of what looks like an ordinary if slightly up-market family home. On the upper floors that is exactly what it is – the residence of city businessman Robert Mynors, his wife Jane and their two children. But to protect its royal pupils the building's windows have been fortified with £20,000 worth of bulletproof glass and other security devices. Local bobbies also regularly patrol the quiet, tree-lined street and move on anyone who loiters too close to the nursery. The children are divided into three classes of twelve – Big Swans, Little Swans and, for the youngest pupils like Harry, the Cygnets. The teachers are all trained in the Montessori method and Harry will not only be learning to count and do finger painting but also to hang his coat neatly on the peg that bears his name and put away toys when he has finished playing with them.

At present the little prince remains an unknown quantity to the world at large. No matter how intelligent or talented he becomes Harry is destined to live forever in the shadow of his more important, older brother. But royal staff who work closely with the ginger-haired royal tot believe he will carve out his own special niche in life.

'He is very advanced for his age,' says one Palace worker. 'In fact, he is much brighter than William was at the same stage. Of course, he is totally different from his brother. He's rather reserved, like his dad, and he always thinks before he says anything.

'William is the exact opposite just like his mother, who always seems to say the first thing that pops into her head.'

During his first term at nursery school Harry will go to classes only for two-and-a-half hours two mornings a week. His big brother is at Wetherby all day and will stay at the £785 pre-preparatory school for the next three years. But his father will be a lot happier when both his sons are attending lessons full-time every day.

He is sometimes disturbed while working at home by the ear-splitting shrieks of his sons playing upstairs in the attic nursery at Kensington Palace. On these occasions he feels it's necessary to go out to escape the noise created by his playful princes.

Once he fled to Clarence House to lunch with the Queen Mother three times in one week. And as he walked into the quiet comfort of his grandmother's residence in the Mall he told her staff: 'I love William and Harry dearly, but sometimes I just have to get away from home to get some peace.'

Some months later while visiting the Great Ormond Street Hospital for Sick Children he let slip another indication of his feelings about mischievous William, then aged four and three-quarters. When he stopped to admire a two-week-old patient, Katie Edwards from Islington, London, he said to her mother Pauline: 'Isn't she adorable? They are so sweet at that age, but wait until they grow a bit. I have discovered I don't like four-year-olds.' However, Charles laughed as much as his wife did when William came home from school bursting to tell them his very first joke. He told it between fits of giggles but his father was pleased to see that his son had inherited a sense of humour.

'Why can't you tell a snake a joke?' William asked his parents. 'I don't know, I give up,' both replied after suggesting some totally unsuitable answers to keep the fun going. William decided to enlighten them. 'Because you can't pull its leg!' he screamed and fell about laughing at his own joke.

Despite the new regime in the royal nursery William did not become angelic overnight. Soon after he started school he was sent home early one day. His mother went out of her way to explain to reporters she met that William had been suffering from a cold. But some Kensington Palace aides claimed he was whisked away from his class because he had thrown a temper tantrum and his teachers simply could not control him.

William is seen being disciplined now on other occasions too. He and his little brother Harry were taken to watch their father playing polo one Sunday afternoon in May 1987. William cheered as his dad scored two goals for his team the Maple Leafs. At the end of the afternoon he decided to dash out on to the pitch to join his father in the prize-winners' line-up. Ruth Wallace's deputy Olga Powell, who was on duty that weekend, grabbed the little runaway and hauled him back. William desperately tried to wriggle out of her clutches but awesome Olga firmly ordered him to behave.

The royal scamp burst into tears as he got a public ticking off. Significantly, his mother, sitting some distance away, called him over to her and dried his tears with a kiss. It was proof once again that Diana is an easy-going mum. And having grown up with an energetic little brother Charles, who is three years younger than herself, she knows what little boys can get up to.

But the more Prince Charles learns about little boys the more he yearns to have a daughter. He often tells members of his Household staff who have little girls that they are lucky. 'Girls are so much nicer than boys, don't you think?' he asked one father of two teenage daughters.

The Prince is especially fond of his little neighbours Davina, who is nine, and Rose Gloucester, seven, the daughters of his cousin Richard, Duke of Gloucester. The Gloucester girls are dainty little blondes who love frilly dresses and hate getting dirty. During half-term holidays they rush out to watch Prince Charles take off for official engagements from the helipad in the grounds of Kensington Palace. Before he climbs aboard his chopper the Prince always stops to scoop the girls up into his arms for a goodbye kiss.

Initially, Charles was ecstatic about being a father. He read dozens of books on baby care and attended a lecture on the father's role in childbirth to prepare for his first child's arrival. When Prince William was born on 21 June 1982 at 9.03 p.m. he was with his wife in the delivery room of the private Lindo Wing of St Mary's Hospital, Paddington.

Two hours afterwards when a beaming Charles emerged from the hospital my colleague Harry Arnold and I were the first to congratulate him. He told us he was overwhelmed by the experience of seeing his son's arrival into the world. 'It's a very adult thing to do,' he explained a bit obscurely.

'Is the baby like you, Sir?' I asked.

'Fortunately, no,' he answered with a chuckle. His son had fair hair, sort of blondish and blue eyes, he announced. When Harry informed him that the delighted crowd outside the hospital had been singing 'Nice one, Charlie, nice one son, now give us another one,' the Prince reacted with mock amazement. 'Bloody Hell! Give us a chance.' Then he added grinning: 'Better ask my wife. I don't think she'd be too pleased about that just yet.' Then turning to me he said that Diana was very tired and he was worried about the noise of the celebrations in the street disturbing her. 'Some sleep is urgently needed,' he explained.

None of us who were there reporting the birth of another heir to the throne that night had ever seen the Prince of Wales so happy. He was still smiling broadly when he returned to see his wife and baby before nine o'clock the following morning. Later the same day the Princess's doctor declared that she was in such good shape she could take her baby home where they would be far more comfortable.

At six o'clock that evening the new parents walked slowly down the front steps of the Lindo Wing with Charles holding his son snugly wrapped in a lacy shawl. The crowds who had been lining the street all day got only a glimpse of a white bundle as the royal couple posed for the gang of photographers lined up on the opposite pavement. The *Sun* newspaper arranged for one of their cameramen to climb a high wall and shoot down on the little family thus gaining the only clear shot of the new baby's face. With his eyes tightly shut and one finger in his mouth the as yet unnamed little prince slept soundly in his father's arms, unaware that he was meeting the press for the very first time.

Back home at Kensington Palace Charles and Diana tried to decide on names for the newborn. She was keen on names like Oliver and Rupert which were currently fashionable among her friends in the Sloane Ranger set. Her husband preferred good, old-fashioned family names like George. They finally compromised by choosing William because, Charles explained afterwards, he himself did not have a close relative with that name.

Ten days after her son was born Diana celebrated her twenty-first birthday. Before this milestone she had become the world's favourite covergirl, married the most eligible man on earth and given him a son and heir. As she recovered at home Princess Diana had good reason to celebrate.

Three days earlier Buckingham Palace had announced that her son would be named William Arthur Philip Louis and known as Prince William of Wales.

The delay in announcing the new Prince's name led to furious business in betting shops around the country. The bookmakers lost heavily when one shrewd punter made a killing with the winning name. As a result there were angry mutters about leaks from royal relatives providing inside information.

To avoid a repetition of this fuss the Prince and Princess had another name ready when their second son Prince Henry Charles Albert David was born on 15 September 1984. But to his family and the world at large, he would be known simply as Prince Harry, royal press officer Victor Chapman told the reporters assembled outside the hospital.

To make the announcement official a notice bearing the names of the infant Prince had to be posted, as tradition demanded, in the forecourt of Buckingham Palace. Prince Charles' private secretary at the time, Edward Adeane, decided he had better organise this as quickly as possible. The street outside the hospital was jammed with spectators, police and press but the royal aide asked for a car to be brought to the door immediately to take him to the Palace.

After a behind-the-scenes flap a driver was found and a car eventually brought to the door, and the flustered Adeane departed. But when he reached Buckingham Palace he found a crowd outside the gates celebrating the royal birth barred his way. When a zealous police officer attempted to turn his unmarked car away Adeane began yelling above the cheering spectators trying to explain who he was and why he had to gain entry.

The more he urged his driver to keep the car moving forward the more determined the police seemed to keep him out. The nearest officer happened to be struggling to control a police dog on a tight leash as Adeane thundered that the man had to let him through at once. At that moment the crowd pressed forward and the over-excited dog leapt up and bit a ten-year-old boy standing nearby. Chaos ensued as the child screamed, and the police officer yelled urgently for assistance, while Adeane, cursing his luck, was forced to back away from the Palace gates.

It was not until some time later that a neatly typed statement was clipped to the Palace noticeboard bearing the names chosen for Charles and Diana's second son.

Once again overwhelmed with the joys of fatherhood the Prince decided to cut down on his official duties and spend more time with his family. For the first year of Harry's life he was as involved with him as Diana, who commented dryly: 'My husband knows so much about rearing children that I've suggested he has the next one and I'll sit back and give advice.'

When the new baby was six months old Diana was forcibly reminded that her wishes as a mother sometimes had to give way to the needs of the Crown. The Prince and Princess had decided to take their children to Scotland for a quiet weekend break in March 1985. It was the first time baby Harry had flown with his parents and the Queen made it clear she would not permit Charles and his sons to travel in the same aircraft. She feared one tragic accident might rob the throne of the three male heirs in direct line of succession.

Previously Charles had flown several times with Prince William, but suddenly permission was withdrawn. So the wide-eyed toddler flew from London to Aberdeen with his nanny on an ordinary scheduled flight, while his baby brother travelled with his parents on a royal Andover.

The Queen has always stuck to a firm rule that she will never travel with Charles and in turn, before his marriage, he would not fly with his brother Andrew.

But after the birth of Prince William the Queen relaxed the ban on her heirs flying together when the baby Prince left Britain to accompany his parents on a tour of Australia and New Zealand in 1983.

He was not quite nine months old and on the long flight needed the comfort of both his mother and his father, Diana argued. She got her way. But after Prince Harry was born the Queen insisted that it was far too risky for the whole family to travel together.

The Princess did not share her mother-in-law's fears. First of all, she argued, air travel today is a far safer form of transport than driving on British roads and aircraft of the Queen's flight are more scrupulously inspected and serviced than almost any others in the air. The chances of an accident befalling the Royal Family are therefore much lower than average.

But even more than these practical arguments Diana wanted her children to jet away on holiday with both their parents just like any ordinary family. It annoyed her that they couldn't necessarily do so.

Once again Prince Charles found himself the man in the middle, torn between the opposing views of the two women he loved most – his wife and his mother.

Protracted arguments followed the first separate flights for Prince Charles and Prince William. But in 1986 Diana surprised everyone by triumphantly flying off with her husband and sons for a seaside holiday in Majorca. 'Finally, the Princess won her husband over to her side,' reveals a friend of the family. 'Prince Charles has decided the advantages of flying as a family group outweigh the risks of an appalling accident – at least, while his children are small and not flying very often. The cost of separate flights for young William, his nanny and a detective helped to tip the balance. The Prince always loves a chance to save money so he persuaded the Queen to agree.'

Prince Charles is not so much concerned about the way his sons travel as the direction in which they are heading. It is his responsibility to chart the course of the Crown into the twenty-first century. His heirs will fly in space yet must uphold the traditions of a medieval monarchy. In particular, his elder son must understand the language of computer technology while uttering ancient vows at his Coronation. Preparing one small boy for this strange destiny is a formidable task. But Charles is very much aware that nothing he achieves will be as important as training William to take on this sacred trust.

7

The Royal Order of the Boot

Working for the world's favourite royals may seem like a dream job. But only a handful of the people who were with Prince Charles in his bachelor days are still on his staff. At least twenty-five employees moved on in the first six years after Charles and Diana were married.

Inevitably, this has led many people to suspect that the atmosphere around the Prince and Princess of Wales is strained and staff do not enjoy their work.

Of course, some employees have left of their own accord. But many more, it is rumoured, received the Royal Order of the Boot. The high turnover of staff at Highgrove and Kensington Palace began soon after the Prince and Princess became engaged in February 1981. As a result, many people suspected that Princess Diana was responsible.

To squash these rumours Diana approached a *Daily Mirror* journalist who had blamed her for yet another royal employee's departure. 'I want you to understand I don't sack people,' she told him angrily. Unfortunately, few people believed her. And reports kept circulating that determined Diana wore the pants in her family.

Inside Kensington Palace everyone knows that only one person is in charge and it is Prince Charles. He may seem a kind and gentle man but he has no qualms about shouting at anyone who annoys him. His word is final in his own home and every member of the Royal Household refers to him as 'the Boss'.

His late valet Stephen Barry used to say it was never advisable to speak to any member of the Royal Family before eleven o'clock in the morning because they were all grumpy until then.

Despite his soft-hearted image Prince Charles can be steely in making sure he gets what he wants. His present valet, Ken Stronach, is often on the receiving end of early morning grumbles. Charles likes to dress in a hurry, and a tie or a belt left in the wrong place may be tossed across the room. But the Prince's staff report that his bad moods never last long.

Inefficiency and delays are always certain to bring out his bad temper. And anyone who has ever been on the receiving end of a dressing down from the Prince of Wales is never likely to forget it. The signs of royal fury are always easily spotted. Charles gets twitchy, then begins muttering 'I don't know why I bother,' a favourite expression that means somebody has upset him. The Prince of Wales does not like to be messed about or kept waiting. Repeated offences are sure to put anyone on his black list.

For obvious reasons the Prince, like the Queen, tries not to let anyone know that he sacks people. If he is dissatisfied with someone he just freezes them out. A few months of cool treatment usually makes someone realise that they have fallen from favour. Quite often, they take the hint and resign.

If this doesn't work he makes arrangements for someone else to do the dirty work. He is so successful at these indirect dismissals that some people go to him complaining that a top royal aide has given them notice to quit and ask him to intervene.

Prince Charles is always sympathetic and says: 'I'll see what I can do,' but the employee ends up going. This diplomatic form of sacking prevents a lot of unpleasantness.

It is often difficult for royal employers to hire the right people because you can't live like a king on the wages, but the perks are truly palatial. The Princess's chief lady-in-waiting, Anne Beckwith-Smith, wears a diamond-studded brooch in the shape of the initial 'D' – a gift from her grateful boss. And Diana's maid, Evelyn Dagley, has often been spotted whizzing off on shopping trips in the Princess's own zippy little sports car.

Joining the royal payroll seems like a red carpet ride through life. Private jets, helicopters and Jaguars are always waiting to whisk staff off with their bosses to the splendid royal estates. While some, like ladies-in-waiting, live out, maids, cooks and valets get board and lodging at some of the best addresses in the world.

The Queen has also built holiday cottages for staff on all her estates. This means that chauffeurs and domestics who travel up from London to Scotland in the summer with the Prince and Princess of Wales can take their families with them so their job becomes a working holiday. And during their time off they can make use of comfortable accommodation at Windsor or Sandringham. Balmoral has a nine-hole golf course which all royal employees are invited to use and royal cars are always available for their use when off duty.

Whenever they are required to stay at isolated places like Balmoral or Sandringham a staff bar is provided with cut-price drinks for off-duty hours. They are so well patronised that both the Queen and Princess Diana have sometimes been kept awake by staff enjoying late-night drinking sessions.

Because these country estates are tucked away miles from the nearest town the Royals feel they must provide some fun for their workers. So first release movies are also screened each week.

Prince Charles once turned up to claim his front row seat at Balmoral Castle only to find a servant who had been a trifle too long in the bar had bagged it and refused to shift. With good grace the Prince caved in to the 'first come' principle and found a seat at the back.

At the ghillies balls and fancy dress parties held each summer in the Royal Family's Highland home cooks and carpenters can boogie with Princess Diana or rock and reel with Fergie. The whole family also throws a staff Christmas party where they wait on the people who normally wait on them.

Every employee receives a gift at a special presentation just before Diana and Charles leave London to celebrate Christmas with the Queen at Windsor. No one is forgotten from top aides right down to the newest scullery maid. These presents range in value from hardback books to crystal decanters and porcelain.

Staff who give personal service are always cared for in their old age. Prince Charles' former nanny Mabel Anderson lived rent free in a charming grace and favour house on the Duchy of Cornwall estate in south London until she died in 1987.

Charles and Diana also threw a lunch party at a Gloucestershire hotel when Paddy Whiteland, their odd-job man at Highgrove, turned seventy in 1984. And when Paddy's wife Nesta died of cancer two years later Princess Diana interrupted a holiday in Scotland to travel back to Highgrove for the funeral. Afterwards the Princess took the grief-stricken old man back to Balmoral for a complete break and sat with him for hours each day helping him to cope with his loss.

Such consideration is worth far more to many people than high wages. No one would get rich working for Charles and Diana. The pay is notoriously low and the hours are often long. Many domestic staff earn well under £100 a week but they get free board and lodging. Ladies-in-waiting are unpaid but receive a small amount for expenses.

Faithful royal retainers believe their low pay is more than outweighed by the immense prestige of living and working with the future king and queen. And when they quit they are always guaranteed good jobs with employers who are impressed by their royal service.

Yet one by one from detectives to domestics Charles and Diana's staff keep walking out. It appears that working for the world's most famous couple is not quite as glamorous as it seems.

First to move on after the Prince became engaged to Lady Diana Spencer was Chief Inspector Paul Officer. His departure was a surprise because he had been with Charles for many years. The Prince valued his services especially after the royal bodyguard saved his life during an incident in 1974 when the Prince was serving in the Royal Navy.

Charles was asleep in the naval barracks at Portland, Dorset, when another lieutenant, with a history of mental illness, went berserk with a knife. He broke into the Prince's private quarters and was confronted by a startled Charles who had been awakened by the noise. The crazed Navy officer was just about to bring a chair crashing down on the Prince's head when Officer rushed into the room and wrestled the attacker to the ground. Prince Charles never forgot this drama and it was a measure of his concern for the safety of his bride-to-be that he asked for Chief Inspector Officer to be assigned to her.

Unaccustomed to a policeman forever hovering at her elbow Diana found it difficult to adjust at first. She got annoyed when Officer took the wheel instead of letting her drive when they went out.

Meanwhile, her shadow realised that he preferred working for a man and did not fancy playing nursemaid to a royal novice, so he asked for a transfer. He left his royal job on the morning the Prince and Princess were married and was put in charge of a south London police station.

Nevertheless, Di's grumbles about Officer Officer leaked out and led to the idea that anyone who displeased her would not last long. It certainly seemed that she was behind the resignation of Charles' valet Stephen Barry. The true story of his departure was much more complicated.

Stephen Barry began working at Buckingham Palace in 1967 as a footman in the royal nursery and became Prince Charles' valet three years later. He stayed with the Prince for twelve years and was much more than an ordinary manservant. He kept Charles' petty cash for incidental expenses, he did his shopping and looked after his private papers, catalogued his photograph albums and turned all his books into a proper library. He helped the Prince move into Highgrove, bought furnishings and even cooked for him when they camped out in the house while it was being renovated.

But most amazing of all, he had the rare privilege of accompanying Charles on many public duties. In fact, he was treated more like an aide than a servant.

But after the royal couple were married their household

increased and other people began to take over the personal services the valet had once provided. Barry no longer went into the bedroom to wake the Prince each morning and bring his breakfast. The Prince and Princess wanted to be left alone together. Diana now picked out the suit, shirt and tie she thought her husband should wear and she also chose the menus for meals. Stephen Barry soon realised that he had far less work to do and far less influence.

Always a conservative dresser, Prince Charles had for years relied on his valet to buy the rather old-fashioned clothes he preferred. But Princess Diana decided that her husband's wardrobe needed smartening up. She went out shopping for brighter shirts and ties and persuaded him to give up wearing his expensive hand-made shoes and switch to Gucci slip-ons.

Naturally, many people suspected that Barry resented this interference. But when he left he insisted that he and the Princess had not had a row. This was true. His departure had more to do with his colourful personal life.

Prince Charles had been aware for some time that his valet was showing signs of behaving much too grandly for a servant. Barry regularly borrowed the Prince's Aston Martin sports car for outings. 'He used to phone for a car to be sent around to the Grand Entrance Portico at Buckingham Palace as if it was for Prince Charles and then drive off in it himself just like one of the Royals,' an amazed footman later revealed. Barry also was in the habit of ordering the royal box at Covent Garden for nights at the opera with his own friends.

He became so high-handed that he made the mistake of trying to tell the royal newcomer how to do her job. He used to cough disapprovingly if she seemed about to make a blunder and raise an eyebrow if she giggled. Prince Charles noted his patronising manner.

Stephen Barry also had an unfortunate habit of making the gossip columns which disturbed some Palace officials. He had been involved in an unseemly scuffle with several gentlemen of uncertain gender in a gay club. From then on his days at the Palace were numbered. The big freeze had begun.

When the royal couple returned from their honeymoon Barry told them of his decision to leave. He did not relish spending much of the time at the Prince and Princess's country home Highgrove, a hundred miles away from the London nightspots he loved.

But when he resigned and gave up his rooms at Buckingham Palace the Prince asked if he would like to have a two-bedroom flat rent-free on the Duchy of Cornwall estate in Kennington, south London. He also presented his former valet with a valuable silver paper knife with the Prince of Wales feathers set in gold in the handle.

Stephen Barry worked in public relations for a while then wrote a book about his years with the Prince, which made a small fortune from overseas sales, although it was banned from publication in Britain.

To promote his writing career he spent a large part of his profits travelling around America and it is there, friends suspect, that he caught the fatal disease Aids. He returned to London for treatment and died in October 1986 aged thirty-seven. Prince Charles was deeply affected when he heard this sad news. He mentioned to several people that he often wondered if Barry's fate would have been different had he stayed on in royal service. The royal servant might not have spent so much time in the United States and perhaps remained a healthy man.

Charles wrote a letter to Barry's sister expressing his deep feelings of sympathy, and since then has taken a keen interest in the work of the Terrence Higgins Trust which assists Aids sufferers.

One new staff member who took over many of Stephen Barry's former duties was Charles and Diana's first butler. Alan Fisher had been Bing Crosby's manservant and also worked for the Duke and Duchess of Windsor. In 1982 when he joined the Wales household he expected they would entertain in the same lavish style as his previous employers. But when he found he had made a mistake, he left in 1984 saying he wanted to return to a more exciting job in America.

The next top employee to become dissatisfied and resign was former diplomat Oliver Everett. He became the Princess's private secretary in 1981 after four years as the Prince's assistant private secretary.

The amount of mail pouring into the Palace more than doubled after Diana's arrival and increased his already heavy workload. On top of this, he felt that the Prince and Princess were creating extra unnecessary work for him by often making last minute changes to their schedule. He tried without success to persuade them both to become more organised. But in 1983 when he heard that Lieutenant Colonel Philip Creasy had been appointed comptroller of the household, a job he had effectively been doing without the title or extra pay, it was the final straw. He left to work as the Queen's deputy librarian at Windsor.

His replacement did not last long. The staff dubbed Creasy 'Colonel Bossy Boots' after he lined them up and gave them orders like an officer addressing his troops. His stiff and starchy ways also seem to have irritated the royal couple who prefer a more relaxed atmosphere in their home. The Colonel soon joined the growing list of ex-royal employees.

The Honourable Edward Adeane, Prince Charles' private secretary, was perhaps the greatest loss of all. His family had served the monarchy for generations. His father Lord Adeane had been principal private secretary to the Queen and before that assistant private secretary to her father King George VI. His great grandfather Lord Stamfordham became assistant private secretary to Queen Victoria in 1880 and later transferred to the staff of the then Duke of York who eventually became King George V.

Adeane was called to the bar in 1962 and gave up a successful law practice to work for the Prince of Wales. A bachelor, he shared Charles' love of shooting and fishing, and he had hoped to remain his top adviser when he became king. But after six years he got fed up with Charles' unbusinesslike attitude to his royal role.

He was often summoned to see the Prince and then kept

waiting for hours outside Charles' study for no good reason. Finally, he decided the job was not right for him and took up work as a barrister again.

The Fall of the House of Adeane from royal favour was a significant defeat for the old guard at the Palace. Like his father before him Edward Adeane was a traditional courtier who knew the form. He belonged to an enclosed world as wary of outside influences as a medieval monastery.

He believed sincerely that Prince Charles should continue to steer the monarchy along the same, safe lines it had always followed and only very gradually adapt to changing times.

Prince Charles was not so sure. And he was encouraged in this attitude by new-style courtiers like Sir Laurens van der Post. The Prince's decision to break away from the aloof style of royalty and go out to see what life was really like in a world where there were no red carpets or fresh paint led him to make secret visits to London's down-and-outs.

He saw for himself homeless people huddled for shelter under the arches of Charing Cross station on London's Embankment. He drove around Finsbury Park to meet other vagrants, and on a similar trip to Camden Town talked to a group of young people living in a squat. Impressed by his concern they offered him a cup of tea but looking around at the lack of modern conveniences he thanked them politely and said he wasn't thirsty.

He also mucked in as a farmhand on several Duchy of Cornwall estates. The Queen, a dedicated follower of the old guard system, would never have dreamed of considering such 'infra dig' schemes.

Some top Palace advisers thought the Prince was acting on 'unsound' advice from people who were too progressive. And the fact that Prince Charles sometimes heeded their advice rather than that of his own staff caused disquiet.

At the time of Adeane's departure some newspapers claimed that he was the victim of a personality clash with Princess Diana, but this was totally untrue. The real reason for Edward Adeane's resignation was his unresolvable differences with

Prince Charles. Diana and Adeane have remained on very friendly terms and still meet occasionally.

Finding a new private secretary for the Prince proved difficult. The head of the Foreign Office, Sir Anthony Acland, was asked to choose one of his outstanding diplomats but many men of the right calibre who were approached turned the job down.

The Prince of Wales' office seemed rather rudderless at the end of 1984 and well into 1985 because Michael Colborne, who looked after Charles and Diana's financial affairs, had resigned shortly before Edward Adeane. The official reason given was he 'wanted a change' but actually the unhappy atmosphere and lack of organisation in the Prince's office was a contributory factor.

Colborne had met the Prince when they served together on the guided missile destroyer *HMS Norfolk.* The former Chief Petty Officer resigned in the summer of 1984, but Charles pleaded with him to stay. 'Too many people have left,' he explained. 'Please reconsider.' After lengthy talks Michael Colborne agreed to stay on until Diana's second baby was born the following September. Then he took up a top management position in the City.

His job was filled by David Roycroft who later took on Edward Adeane's duties when he left. But he was disappointed that he was not confirmed in this important job so he left to become a senior executive at Independent Television News.

Sir John Riddell, an international banker, then became the Prince's private secretary. At the time of his royal appointment he was Executive Director of Credit Suisse-First Boston. A Northumbrian baronet, who married the daughter of the Governor of the Bank of England, he once cherished hopes of entering the House of Commons. He was an unsuccessful Conservative candidate in both the spring and autumn elections of 1974. An old Etonian, he was also Deputy Chairman of the Independent Broadcasting Authority when he joined the Royal Household.

Riddell, who had no previous royal connections, is believed to have gained his prestigious post on the recommendation of mutual friends. His selection seemed further evidence that

Prince Charles wished to distance himself from the old-style courtiers who surround his mother.

With three young children, Sir John tries to ensure that his family life does not suffer too much as a result of his royal duties. For this reason he does not accompany the Prince on all overseas tours as Edward Adeane always did. He frequently sends his deputy instead.

But within months of joining the Palace, other staff noted that Charles' top man seemed to feel thwarted in his new job. Frequently ignoring the advice he pays for, the Prince continues to go his own way.

The post of number two in the Royal Household vacated by Michael Colborne was eventually filled by former Army officer Humphrey Mews in August 1986. He was on loan to the Cabinet Office from the Ministry of Defence with the rank of Colonel when recommended for the job. A bachelor who at times seems more regal than the Prince of Wales, he did not endear himself to the press on Charles' tour of southern Africa the following year. He was responsible for recording all the Prince's speeches in the absence of the press officer's clerk who usually does this job. However, he managed to miss sections of some speeches and on one occasion left his tape recorder behind. Journalists covering each event were asked to come to the rescue; Mr Mews did not seem very grateful for their help.

More popular with his Palace colleagues is the twenty-six-year-old Rupert Fairfax, who left a top post in the City with the Hanson Trust to become Prince Charles' special adviser on industry. He made such a great impression in his first year with his royal boss that he is tipped to take on much wider responsibilities in the future.

Detective Inspector David Robinson was another royal minder who also moved on. After less than a year Diana began complaining that his over-protective style was 'too jumpy' and made her feel nervous. Robinson disliked the constant shopping trips the Princess enjoyed and so he requested a new post. He switched to guarding Princess Anne temporarily and then moved on to Prince Philip's staff.

Sergeant Barry Mannakee's disappearance from Diana's side was more mysterious. Initially he had worked as a 'back-up' to more senior officers protecting the Princess. But Diana was impressed with his work and suggested him when an opening as Prince William's bodyguard came up.

Scotland Yard's Royal Protection Squad is an élite group of officers whose loyalty is unquestioned. Every man is ready at any moment to face any threat. But Diana's minders seem more dedicated than most. They are known as the luckiest men in Britain because they spend so much time with everyone's favourite Princess.

In the summer of 1985 the Princess found herself left alone much of the time while Prince Charles was out stalking on the Balmoral estate. To fill in the empty hours she spent a lot of time driving around the local scenery. Sergeant Mannakee often accompanied her.

Once when zooming along the road from Braemar they passed the turn-off to Balmoral Castle and continued on beyond the next town Ballater. A photographer driving in the same direction to Aberdeen spotted them thirty miles from the castle. When the Princess noticed him coming up fast behind them she slammed on the brakes, did an amazing handbrake turn and drove off back the way she had come. It seemed a peculiar reaction but the freelance lensman thought no more of it at the time.

Although Mannakee held a relatively junior position he seemed more popular with the Princess than many older and more senior members of her staff. This caused some resentment and a few months later Barry Mannakee moved on.

A Scotland Yard spokesman said he had been transferred to duties with the Diplomatic Protection Squad at his own request. But newspapers reported at the time that he had been guilty of 'over-familiarity' with the Princess.

The sergeant, who had a wife Susan and two children, would say only: 'I was transferred for domestic reasons – the job meant long hours away from home.' He added: 'My own reasons are personal and I have no intention of discussing them.'

He was as good as his word. But one of his close friends later revealed that he had been moved on for a professional blunder totally unconnected with the Princess. Tragically in May 1987 Barry Mannakee was killed in a motorbike accident. He was a pillion passenger on a machine driven by a police colleague which was in a collision in east London.

Prince Charles was deeply upset when he learned of the accident the next day and he broke the news to his wife as they left London to attend the Cannes Film Festival. A wreath from both the Prince and Princess was sent to the funeral.

Although some staff have left because they fell out of favour or were disenchanted with conditions at the Palace, others have had personal reasons unconnected with the royal couple.

Chief Inspector John MacLean was Prince Charles' Scotland Yard protection officer for eleven years. The stocky Scotsman was an expert skier and always looked forward to the Prince's winter holidays in the Swiss Alps when he would leave everyone else in the royal party far behind.

Prince Charles had always enjoyed his blunt and often earthy manner. One story in particular illustrates the special relationship the Prince and the police officer had. One evening, Prince Charles and Officer MacLean were driving through Glasgow in a Range Rover, the Prince at the wheel. The Chief Inspector suddenly pointed down a dark side street and casually remarked: 'My mother lives down there.'

'Does she really?' said Charles. 'Let's pop in and see her.' And at that second he made as if to turn around. MacLean, suspecting that his elderly mother might faint with shock if the Prince of Wales appeared without any warning on her doorstep, looked at his watch with mock seriousness. 'No, I'm afraid we've missed her,' he said. 'She'll be out mugging cripples at this time of night.' The two men roared with laughter as they drove on.

Despite the fact that he sincerely enjoyed his job, John MacLean decided to leave in January 1985. Then in his mid-forties he felt royal protection was a job for a younger man and he wanted to go into business for himself. He managed to get totally away from the stresses of security work and started a ski school in Andorra.

The only person who could reasonably claim that the Princess was the real reason he left royal service was her hairstylist Kevin Shanley. This quiet, well-liked man felt he had unfairly been given the brush-off when the Princess began asking his partner in the Headlines salon, Richard Dalton, to do her hair more often than she summoned him.

Shanley had known Diana since her school days and she had been one of his most faithful clients, following him when he moved around different salons in the West End of London. He created the famous chunky bob with the swept back fringe that put Lady Diana on the world's best-tressed lists. At Diana's suggestion he also began trimming Prince Charles' thinning locks and gave Prince William his very first haircut.

Suddenly the man who had women all over the world desperate to 'Di' their hair was a celebrity. He was invited to give styling exhibitions all around the world.

He joined the royal party on Charles and Diana's first big tour overseas in 1983 but flew back to London half way through the trip Down Under to look after the increased business at his salon. Richard Dalton replaced him and from then on stepped in whenever Shanley went on holiday.

But in 1984 Kevin fell out of favour with his royal client when he refused to put her hair up in a sophisticated style claiming it was far too short. Dalton did the job instead, but Shanley was soon vindicated. When the Princess wore the severe hairdo to the State Opening of Parliament it was much criticised by the public and the press.

Despite this Kevin Shanley discovered that his keen eye was no longer appreciated. 'Suddenly I stopped getting calls from the Palace,' he told me later. 'The reason given was I lived too far from the Palace to make early morning appointments with the Princess. However, dashing in from my home in south London had never been a problem before.'

Not long afterwards the Princess made Dalton her official hairstylist. While the two men remained partners in the same salon, clients claimed the electric atmosphere could make their hair stand on end. 'Dalton never let me forget what had happened,' Shanley said cuttingly. 'He was always talking about Diana. He didn't seem to care how I felt.'

Although the two men had been friends and colleagues for almost ten years Dalton left to become a freelance stylist. 'There are 101 ways of doing her hair and we have been trying various styles,' he said when he got his promotion. 'I am going to make her look totally different every time you see her.'

But the Princess had taken to heart reports that the upswept hairdo he created was a big letdown and she never wore it up again. When Dalton brushed out her curls and created a new page-boy shoulder-length bob the fashion world gave it the thumbs down again. Soon the Princess went back to the old short flicked-back style created by his predecessor Kevin Shanley. Despite what newspapers called these 'Di-sasters' Dalton swept ever higher in royal favour, far from his humble origins in Scotland.

Soon afterwards Kevin Shanley revealed in a Sunday newspaper all the secrets of life at Kensington Palace that he had learned while making Diana a head of style. His former friend never spoke to him again.

Since then Richard Dalton has become even more indispensable to the Princess. He not only advises her how to wear her hair but also helps to choose her clothes.

'He is like some sort of a Svengali,' another member of the Princess's staff revealed. 'He spends hours with her choosing clothes for every occasion and deciding on her total look. Once it was her lady-in-waiting Anne Beckwith-Smith that she turned to for advice, but now she only listens to this shampooist. The trouble is his taste is very high camp and theatrical. He is the man responsible for the Dynasty Di look which makes the Princess look like some sort of plastic Hollywood soap star.'

The man who learned his trade in an obscure Edinburgh salon now swans around the world first class with his client. Working freelance enables him to be available

Princess Diana needs him. He quite often visits her four or five times a week, but on tours abroad he may style her hair twice a day.

When Diana asked him to shear off her fluffy hair into a boyish crop in 1986 he was reluctant but eventually gave in. His influence is so powerful that his favourite customer abandoned the style within a month or two and began to grow it longer again just the way Dalton liked it.

Diana and Charles' first chef Roseanna Lloyd left to get married only a few months after she joined their staff. Her delicious dishes had first impressed them when they had dinner at a hotel in Wales where she worked. Soon she was cooking up royal treats for them at Kensington Palace. But the pencil-slim Princess and her husband preferred salads and light meals leaving their chef with so little to do that she happily untied her apron strings to become a farmer's wife back in North Wales.

Major John Winter was an equerry to the Prince for three years before returning to the Parachute Regiment, as he had always planned, in February 1982.

Francis Cornish, who guided the Princess through her first big tour, a six-week slog around Australia and New Zealand in 1983, quit his post as her assistant private secretary the following year. He returned to advance his career as a diplomat in the Foreign Office and became High Commissioner in Brunei.

Lieutenant Commander Peter Eberle became Diana's equerry in October 1983 as her official workload grew too much for her staff to handle. But he was only on secondment from the Royal Navy and returned to sea in 1986. He was replaced by Lieutenant Commander Richard Aylard.

Valerie Gibbs, a maid who worked with the Princess's dresser Evelyn Dagley, was hired soon after Diana began official duties. But in August 1984 she left Kensington Palace to get married complaining that she could not stand the stress of her job.

Another maid decided to look for a new job after being

ordered not to bring boyfriends back to her quarters at Kensington Palace. The ban was slapped on her and another live-in maid. The girls were accustomed to spending their time off drinking in local pubs. But Prince Charles' chief bodyguard Inspector Colin Trimming was concerned that strangers were entering the Palace without any security clearance. And he insisted that the girls obey a 10.30 p.m. curfew for extra safety. Both of them left soon afterwards.

John Clarke and Joe Last, two chauffeurs who left the Army to work for the Prince, left after a row about work rotas at the Palace. The two NCOs left the Forces to work full-time for the heir to the throne but lasted only two years in their new jobs.

And a Kensington Palace cleaner, Sheila Tilly, was among several domestic staff who quit after behind-the-scenes bust-ups with more senior staff.

Royal nanny Barbara Barnes resigned after she realised that a gulf had opened up between her and Prince Charles. She had joined the Prince and Princess's household shortly before Prince William was born and became totally devoted to him. But Charles felt his son lacked discipline and considered Barbara indulged his son too much. Nanny Barnes suddenly left the royal nursery in January 1987.

She was followed shortly afterwards by chef Graham Newbold who resigned to take up a much better paid job at a tourist hotel in Scotland. His replacement was unmarried so did not rate the married quarters flat which Graham Newbold and his wife had occupied in the Royal Household. This became a storage area near the kitchen. Princess Diana was thrilled about gaining more privacy and space and arranged for her new chef to live out.

Overcrowding has caused many staff problems. In the early years of their marriage many more royal employees lived in the apartment which is small by royal standards. Both Charles and Diana resented the close proximity of domestics and felt their private life suffered.

Office staff at Buckingham Palace were also squashed into a suite of rooms that was totally inadequate. As more computers were introduced to cope with the increased mail and other paperwork the Prince of Wales' office had to find new quarters. In June 1987 the clerical staff were informed they were moving to St James's Palace while the Prince's private secretary and his immediate assistants would stay put.

Conditions are hardly ideal most of the time in royal service but there are compensations. The people who have stuck with Charles and Diana since their marriage are united in their praise of their royal employers. Their feelings were summed up by former royal steward Keith Jury who for three years was a crew member on the Royal Yacht *Britannia*. 'Everyone loved having the Prince and Princess of Wales aboard because unlike the other Royals they tried hard to lighten the load on the staff. Instead of calling for someone to get something for them they would pop down the stairs and get it themselves. They didn't expect anyone ever to wait on them hand and foot.'

Diana had made a hit with everyone on the yacht during her honeymoon cruise through the Mediterranean. She got into the habit of drifting around the ship chatting to members of the crew as they worked and asking questions about their different jobs. 'She was more friendly than any of the other members of the Royal Family. One afternoon she sat in the bar playing the piano for us. As soon as the snooty senior officers heard about this they rushed down to explain that she was not actually supposed to be in the crew's quarters. But Diana said she didn't care, she would go wherever she wanted to. We loved her for that.'

Keith Jury remembers that the Princess was always cracking gags. Late one afternoon on a tour of Canada she came back aboard ship looking tired and thirsty. The minute she disappeared from public view she began wrenching at her blue hat. 'I can't wait to get this off,' she announced. 'And I'd love a drink before dinner. I think I'll have a Pimms. I got addicted to them on my honeymoon, you know.' Then with an impish grin she added quickly: 'But that's the only thing I got addicted to.'

A senior member of the royal couple's staff claims that the great attraction of royal service is that Charles and Diana are

are always such good company. 'I remember once when we were on a tour of America and driving through the suburbs of Washington. Our car stopped at a red traffic light and the Prince noticed a big drive-in branch of the Kentucky Fried Chicken chain. He was interested in it because he had never seen one of these drive-in fast food places before.

'He has never been keen on what are known as junk foods and something he noticed outside the restaurant made him laugh. A chicken leg had been dropped on the pavement and a small dog was sniffing it. As we turned to look we saw the puppy turn its nose up as if it didn't like the chicken much.

'The Prince pointed at it and joked: "There you are, not even a dog will eat the Colonel's chicken."'

In general, the people who work for him regard Prince Charles as a considerate and good-natured boss. But many members of the Royal Household believe that more staff will continue to leave his service while he remains uncertain of what he wants to do with his life. Until the king-in-waiting finds some sort of fulfilling role many of those around him feel there is not much satisfaction to be gained working for him.

8

The Royals and the Rat Pack

The royal leak Prince Charles has always dreaded most will never appear in the press if he can help it.

Like any other man he occasionally gets caught short a long way from home. It usually happens when he spends hours casting for salmon in the River Dee at Balmoral.

But after a lifetime looking over his shoulder to check if a lens is peeping out from behind a bush the Prince has learned how to keep at least one intimate secret under wraps.

He proved this when a pompous American reporter once asked if he ever got fed up with Fleet Street's newshounds forever snapping at his heels. After a minute's thought Charles grinned. 'Actually, they don't really bother me at all,' he admitted. 'The only time I worry when they are around is when I'm up at Balmoral fishing. When I'm standing in the river for hours I sometimes have a pee in the water. And I'm always petrified some cameraman is going to catch me at it.'

The odd relationship between the Royal Family and the Rat Pack, as the reporters and photographers who cover them are known, has always been far more good-natured than the general public imagines.

Quite often when stepping off a plane or out of a car into yet another sea of strange faces, the Prince seeks out the familiar band of pressmen waiting for him and stops for a friendly word. This is especially true when Royals and journalists are thrown together on foreign tours. Almost all royal expeditions overseas begin with a cocktail party intended to introduce the VIP to the journalists who will be reporting the visit.

Both Prince Charles and his wife enjoy seizing this chance to score points off the press in friendly exchanges. The Princess loves to tease the men who pursue her for a living about their freebie trips around the world, and she often fishes for compliments to reassure herself that she is still their number one quarry. 'Oh, you don't need me any more now that you've got Fergie, do you?' she often says pretending to pout. But she looks thoroughly pleased when they disagree with her.

Diana loves the colourful bunch of characters who pursue her and enjoys overhearing snatches of their special lingo as they work. The Rat Pack cameramen don't take photographs of the Royals, they 'whack 'em'. And the pictures that result are 'smudges', a jokey expression meaning they are all out of focus. The snappers are also called 'Monkeys' by the 'scribblers' who work with them. In return the photographers call the top reporters who are their partners their 'caption writers'.

Prince Charles also enjoys a joke with the gang. He was particularly amused when the *Sun's* royal correspondent Harry Arnold replied to criticism that they were nothing but scum with the quip: 'We may be scum, but we're the crème de la scum.'

The Prince, however, likes to use journalists as an information service whenever he gets the opportunity. 'What's all this fuss about Indian brides at Heathrow?' he once asked Harry Arnold. Harry, a sharp operator who has worked in Fleet Street for more than twenty-five years, quickly briefed the Prince. Immigration officers, concerned that some Asian women were entering Britain illegally by posing as the wives of British residents, were arranging virginity tests for all Indian brides, he explained.

'Well, I'm getting so many letters about the subject you'd think I was responsible for doing the tests myself,' Charles joked. Just then his Scotland Yard bodyguard, Chief Inspector John MacLean, butted in.

'Do you mean getting head down with the old miner's lamp, Sir?'

Charles laughed and wagged a finger as a warning to his minder. 'John, you really go too far sometimes.'

Unlike the Queen, the Prince is not at all bothered if anyone breaks the Don't-speak-to-Royals-before-they-speak-to-you rule of royal protocol. Quite frequently on official jobs he pauses in front of a group of pressmen and looks inquiringly at them as if willing to answer any questions they wish to put.

At one encounter in Hong Kong a photographer asked him why he had slagged off British workers in a recent outburst, along the same lines as his father Prince Philip's famous 'Pull your finger out' speech.

'You must have known you'd get a lot of shtick for saying the British are lazy. Why did you do it?' the cameraman asked.

'You know how naive I am,' Charles said. 'I didn't fully understand what I was getting into. Believe me, I won't do that again.'

Palace press officers have no hesitation in admitting that the Royal Family realise only too well that without the media the monarchy would have trouble staying in business. The Queen and her family would prefer to control the publicity they get, but they realise with a free press this is impossible.

At the same time they are slowly learning to put the pressure on now and again so that they can indirectly achieve a somewhat similar result.

A prime example of this was Prince Charles' swift reaction in 1981 when the Archbishop of Canterbury, Dr Robert Runcie, told reporters that he had given Charles and Diana some fatherly advice about sex in marriage. It was 'a good thing given by God which nevertheless, like all God's gifts needs to be directed right,' he reminded them.

Within hours a highly placed member of the Prince's staff was on the telephone to a journalist who had won the Palace's respect for accurate reporting. 'You may not quote me, but you will be interested to know that the Prince of Wales is absolutely livid,' he revealed.

The aide went on to explain that the Prince was horrified that such a very private conversation had been alluded to by a man he trusted. 'The Prince feels that he and Lady Diana were betrayed,' the source explained, adding it was unlikely that the Archbishop would ever gain his confidence again.

Pressmen are frequently criticised for printing wild allegations about members of the Royal Family because 'they can't answer back'. Nonsense. The truth is Royals can and frequently do lash back at stories, true or false, that they don't like.

When any member of the Royal Family wants to set the record straight or knock down a wild rumour they have several different ways at their disposal to do so.

First, they may authorise an official spokesman at the Buckingham Palace press office to issue a denial. But this direct route is sometimes counter-productive because it stirs up even more interest in the original story instead of squashing it.

Therefore, a reply may be 'leaked' via a royal aide trusted to give the authorised version. This usually works well and provides the kind of unattributed stories seen in the popular press that include the phrase 'a top Palace aide revealed last night'.

A problem only arises if the royal confidante is not very experienced at dropping scoops in the right places. He or she may sometimes reveal too much or accidentally distort the facts. This happened in October 1985, when Macclesfield architect Dr Rod Hackney revealed that the Prince had expressed deep fears over what Britain might be like when he came to the throne.

A political storm erupted after the *Daily Mail* published an interview in which Hackney, an adviser on community architecture to the Prince, said: 'He does not want to become king in an atmosphere where there could be no-go areas in our cities. He is particularly concerned that minorities in the inner cities will become alienated.'

Dr Hackney revealed that over dinner aboard the royal train the Prince had asked him to investigate the problem of disenchanted communities in the rundown areas of London and other big cities.

Labour leaders immediately seized the opportunity to attack the Thatcher government over recent inner-city riots. And Downing Street staff contacted Buckingham Palace asking what it was Prince Charles had actually said.

Were the Prince's remarks, as reported by Dr Hackney, an attack by the Royal Family on the government's urban aid strategy?

After checking with Charles, who was on a visit to the state of Victoria in Australia, Court officials hastily assured the Prime Minister's staff that the Prince's comments had been misinterpreted.

Hackney, who had talked of ordinary people 'beginning to cry out from the heart and that they want help now', soon began to modify his earlier statement.

By the following day he denied saying Charles had been worried about no-go areas. The Prince 'does not see it as a divided Britain', he declared. 'As a citizen he is concerned about inner cities as anybody should be.' And in a complete about-turn he added: 'Most of the things I said came from an Institute of Directors speech he made back in February.'

Labour MPs continued to drag out the fuss by harping on the similarity of Charles' comments to the sympathy his great-uncle, the Duke of Windsor, expressed for jobless miners during the pre-World War II depression. Edward, then Prince of Wales, had insisted that 'something must be done' for the poverty-stricken areas of South Wales.

Prince Charles knows only too well that politics is his own personal no-go area and he was horrified that people believed he had entered this controversial arena.

When he met the press on arrival in Melbourne he wasted no time pointing out to them exactly what he thought of any friend who couldn't zip his lip. 'He will be receiving a letter from me about all this,' Charles declared and his expression of barely controlled annoyance made it obvious the architect would not enjoy reading it.

'I've never said Britain is divided and I've never used the phrase: "When I become king" – it's so pompous,' the Prince protested. He added: 'I feel betrayed. This has destroyed everything I have been trying to do in a quiet way for years. The last thing I wanted to do was become involved in a political row.'

It was not the only occasion on which the Prince had an 'off-the-record' chat which he wanted to see in print. At times he goes out of his way to give stories to newspapers and knows better than his own press officer just what is guaranteed a good run in the tabloids.

His six-day tour of southern Africa in March 1987 began less than three weeks after the Zeebrugge ferry disaster. The *Sun* newspaper had immediately organised a Ferry Aid pop record with all profits from the hit going to relatives of the victims. At a hastily arranged recording session more than 100 rock and pop stars joined together to produce a moving new version of the old Beatles hit 'Let It Be'.

On his first stop in Swaziland, while visiting Waterford College in the hills above Mbabane, he walked over to an American student called Ellen Haus who was teaching Swazi schoolkids to play the guitar. Noticing a member of the *Sun*'s staff standing nearby he asked the teenager: 'What song are you teaching the children – is it "Let It Be?"'

Ellen looked completely nonplussed by the question as the Ferry Aid pop record had not reached Africa, but the *Sun* man gratefully noted the Prince's apparently idle remark. In the next edition of the newspaper the Prince's plug for the charity record made front-page news.

He gave the paper famous for its Page Three pin-ups another little line tailor-made for its readership when he saw some busty Kikuyu dancing girls bouncing towards him at Nairobi airport as they performed a ceremonial dance. Pointing out one particularly well-stacked woman he said: 'That's the best test of a bra I've ever seen.'

After thirty-nine years as an international celebrity Charles has learned more about the media than any press officer on his staff. He realises that the vast majority of the Queen's subjects get most of their information about the Royal Family from two main sources – the tabloid press and television. And although he never reads any newspaper except *The Times* he appreciates the publicity he gets in the popular papers – even if the stories are not always very flattering.

Every morning, no matter where he is in the world, his staff give him a summary of the London papers which is telexed or 'faxed' on a facsimile machine overnight from Buckingham Palace. Often the Prince knows before the reporters accompanying him that their reports have appeared in print.

At times it seems the Prince thinks exactly like a newsman and could do the job as well as any Fleet Street pro. After visiting a tea plantation in Kenya in 1987, he stopped at a factory to sample the product. Like an experienced tea taster he took a sip of the bitter, black brew, swilled it around in his mouth and spat it into the spittoon provided.

Journalists, normally not allowed to photograph any member of the Royal Family eating or drinking, decided the sight was just their cup of tea. 'It tastes much better with milk and sugar. This is much too strong,' Charles declared after trying four different blends and promptly spitting spoonfuls of strong Pekoe out again.

Later over lunch he told his staff he knew exactly the caption that was sure to be used with the photographs taken at the factory. 'It's got to be my Spitting Image,' he declared. And sure enough the title of the TV series that savagely pokes fun at the Royal Family appeared underneath his picture the following day.

Prince Andrew, now the Duke of York, could not be more different in his attitude to the press. Although he is a photographer himself and has had many of his pictures published in magazines and newspapers around the world, he seems to have little idea what makes a good, newsy picture.

Hoots of laughter broke out on picture desks all around Fleet Street when Andrew's official photograph of Prince Harry on his first birthday arrived. He had captured Charles and Diana's younger son sitting in a swing on the deck of the Royal Yacht *Britannia* with a rope that secured the swing in front of Harry's face. Several newspaper editors decided the 'severed head' shot was unusable.

Andrew's hostility to many cameramen is probably the result of their hot pursuit during his romance with the American starlet Koo Stark. Many unsympathetic snappers wonder how he could have expected any other treatment when he travelled with her as man and wife on a scheduled airliner en route to a Caribbean holiday in 1982.

Despite camping on Miss Stark's doorstep night and day for months, not one journalist ever succeeded in getting a usable shot of the Prince and the Showgirl. Andrew ducked and dived away from every trap set by the supersleuths of Fleet Street. But winning the game was apparently not good enough. He decided to get his revenge on the royal Rat Pack when he visited California the following year. On a visit to a housing project in Watts, the black ghetto on the outskirts of Los Angeles, he picked up a paint sprayer, aimed it in the direction of the press and pulled the trigger. White emulsion shot out of the nozzle covering journalists standing just a few feet away. 'I enjoyed that,' Andrew chuckled as he dropped the weapon.

But the hot-shot helicopter pilot of the Falklands campaign was not exactly on target. His aim went a little wide and he hit several innocent Americans accredited to follow his tour. The British Consulate later paid out $1800 in compensation for damaged cameras and clothes to the paint-splattered pressmen.

The Rat Pack had miraculously escaped Andrew's spraygun almost unscathed, but they were seething when they encountered the Prince the following evening at a dinner in his honour attended by Hollywood's best-known British actors. In the course of a speech of thanks for his warm welcome to California Andrew made some slighting remarks about the journalists who had come with him. Loud boos erupted from the back of the room where the pressmen were positioned. But actor Michael Caine quickly lightened the atmosphere with a joke. 'Any time you want to come and paint my cabana you've got the job,' he informed Andrew as laughter swept the room.

But members of the Royal Family back home in Britain thought the prankster Prince's antics were no laughing matter. As the Queen Mother later told a group of friends when she visited Venice on the *Britannia*. 'If only he had apologised straight away there would have been much less fuss.'

At the time Andrew was not accompanied by any Palace press officer to advise him about his gaffe. Since then he has not been allowed to set off on a tour without one.

Even when he decides to be friendly to Fleet Street Andrew still manages to put his foot in it. Like many members of his family he is under the impression that photographers make a fortune out of covering the Royal Family. The truth is that all the top cameramen working for national newspapers receive a salary which remains the same whether they cover royal tours, the Law Courts or sports stories. As one man explained to Princess Diana when she teased him about cashing in on her pictures: 'I get the same dough whether I whack you or go down the Old Bailey.'

On a tour of Canada once Andrew asked a very surprised photographer, Ken Lennox, how much he earned. 'I'll tell you if you tell me what you get,' the snapper said, slightly taken aback.

'It's a deal,' the Prince agreed.

He listened closely as Ken, a canny Scot, explained that salaries for photographers in Fleet Street ranged from around £20,000 to £35,000, then added: 'Now how much money do you get?'

Andrew was cagey. 'Well, you know what I get paid. It's all published in the Civil List,' he hedged.

'You're welshing on our deal,' the photographer complained. 'Come on, tell me what you're worth.'

The Prince owned up. 'You know I get £20,000 from the Civil List and my Navy pay is £12,700.' (Both have since risen considerably.)

'Nothing else?' Ken Lennox persisted.

Andrew laughed. 'What do you mean? Is there a pile of money waiting for me when my Granny snuffs it?'

The Queen's second son has always been both wary of and fascinated by Fleet Street's hacks. But it was only when they were both literally in the same boat during the Falklands War that Prince and pressmen really got to know each other. Several reporters shipped out on the warship *HMS Invincible*, on which Prince Andrew was serving as a helicopter pilot, when it sailed for the South Atlantic. Among them was reporter Tony Snow, who was born and raised in Bow, and has the typical East Ender's lack of pretension. After months at sea with the Prince he decided Andrew was a friendly bloke but a bit thick sometimes. The reporter cites one incident aboard ship which explains a lot about the royal war hero.

'In the bowels of the ship there was a café which stayed open round-the-clock,' Snow remembers. 'The pilots used to eat there if they had missed regular meals through flying duties. It's a real Joe's caff that does marvellous fry-ups.

'It was there that I introduced "H" as we all called His Royal Highness, to that East End delicacy the sausage and bacon sandwich. Up to then he had always ordered either bacon or sausage for his snacks.

'During the campaign all pilots were issued with side arms to carry on flights in case they get shot down and have to defend themselves. One night in the café I noticed a big, heavy 45 automatic pistol lying on the counter. I thought someone had rushed off and forgotten it. I mentioned this and Prince Andrew, who was sitting nearby, picked it up and said: "No, it's mine."

'He lifted the pistol, pointing it straight at my chest only about a foot away. I jumped out of range behind a pillar then walked around to the other side of Andrew's seat. He swung around to ask me why I had leaped about so suddenly, unconsciously turning to face me with the pistol still held in front of him aimed straight at me again.

'I couldn't believe that a bloke who had been around guns on royal estates all his life could behave so stupidly. "Point that thing somewhere else," I yelled. "H" looked surprised and said: "Don't worry, it's not loaded."

'Wagging a finger sternly in his face, I warned: "It's always the unloaded gun that goes off and kills someone."

'Then I told him the joke about the man charged with murdering his wife by stabbing her who claimed: "I was cleaning my knife and it went off accidentally." Andrew roared with laughter and put his gun away.'

The Duke of York seems unable to remain on good terms with the press for any length of time, something his wife manages to do effortlessly.

Andrew and Fergie were invited to join the Prince and Princess of Wales on their skiing holiday at the Swiss resort Klosters in February 1987. Arriving a day before their hosts, the Duke and Duchess set off on a railway cabin to reach the mountain-top unaware that a skier, standing only a few feet away as they were lifted up the valley, was a freelance magazine writer.

The royal couple began arguing about their different attitudes to the press and the astounded journalist squashed into the crowded car beside them could not help overhearing every word.

Andrew began by objecting to the dozen or so pressmen who had arrived in Klosters to cover their visit. A little earlier an aide had put to him a deal suggested by the media. If the Royals would agree to a five-minute photo session the journalists would withdraw afterwards, leaving them to enjoy their skiing without harassment. Andrew turned the offer down flat.

As he stepped into the car he gave his wife a nudge and pointing out some people in the next cabin he warned: 'We've got journalists next door.'

The Duchess calmly replied: 'I don't want any trouble or any pushing or shoving. It doesn't reflect well on me.' As Andrew groaned, she went on: 'If they're going to take pictures I want to look my best and not as if I'm hiding. I have a very good relationship with the press and I want to keep it that way.'

Andrew could not be persuaded to cooperate. 'I don't know why you bother – they're just an awful Rat Pack,' he snarled.

His bolshy mood made his wife see red. 'Sometimes you're just like your father,' she snapped back. 'For heaven's sake, they only want to take your photo, not shoot you!'

However, the tiff did not last long. Fergie planted a kiss on her husband's sullen face and added: 'But I love you.'

The frosty atmosphere between the press and the royal skiers thawed next day when Prince Charles arrived and persuaded his brother to see sense and pose for the photographers on the slopes. More than 100 cameramen crowded together jostling for the best angles as Charles and Andrew, Diana and Fergie lined up obligingly to face their lenses. Their rather stiff poses suddenly dissolved as the royal sisters-in-law began pushing and shoving each other just like the photographers they were facing. The Duchess started the knockabout routine when she nudged the Princess and whispered: 'Right, let's have a go.'

Diana played the fall girl by pretending to lose her balance and grabbed her friend for support. The two women began laughing out loud as they slithered about on the piste. But Prince Charles, thinking his wife was in trouble, leaned over to help her up and said coldly: 'Come on, come on.'

After a few minutes the royal foursome skied off down the valley and disappeared into the icy mist. The official Rat Pack went off to wire their pictures and file their stories to their London offices and everyone seemed happy – with the exception of Prince Charles. He was slightly annoyed because the photo call had been arranged for 9.30 a.m. 'I like to be up and out by 8.30 a.m. at the latest,' he grumbled. 'And we've wasted a whole hour on the slopes already.'

Although the Fleet Street newshounds had got what they wanted not all of them returned to England as they had promised. At least two teams from national newspapers left the Princes and their wives alone, but stayed on in Klosters just in case one or other of the royal party had a skiing accident or made news with some other mishap.

Victor Chapman, who arranged the rendezvous on the slippery slopes, said afterwards that he thought the photocall was a great success. Charles and Diana have nicknamed him 'Cecil B. DeMille' after the famous Hollywood producer who staged the most spectacular shots of all time.

But many of the journalists who had been covering Charles' skiing holidays in Klosters for the past eight or nine years disagreed. 'Just about any Wally with an instamatic camera seems to wangle accreditation these days,' one reporter said sadly. 'The whole session has become a bunfight with photographers elbowing each other aside for good positions because there are only a few Royals and around a hundred photographers.

'It was so different when Charles first started going to Klosters. There were only five or six of us who covered the trip then. We never harassed the Prince, but he always gave us good pictures.'

On the trips before Prince Charles got married there were five or six photographers who used to call around at his chalet each evening to ask his staff what the plans were for the next day. As they chatted, the Prince, fresh from the shower with only a towel around his waist, often walked along the hall past them and waved hello. His Scotland Yard police officer would tell the pressmen where they were heading next day so they could get good shots and then after five minutes taking pictures they would leave the Prince in peace for the rest of the day.

'Today it's just a bloody nightmare with paparazzi popping up behind every snowdrift. No wonder the Royals get fed up,' the reporter sighed.

Of course the reason everything has changed is Diana. The snazzy Princess of Wales is a stunning sight on the slopes, so every magazine and newspaper in Europe wants pictures of Diana doing a parallel turn or better still falling flat on her beautiful bottom.

Prince Charles may feel he has paid a high price for having a gorgeous wife.

Jayne Fincher, the only girl photographer who regularly covers the Royal Family, has even fonder memories of Klosters before Charles married Diana. The daughter of the legendary photo-journalist Terry Fincher, Jayne has joined her father in the family firm Photographers International. She had only been shooting the Queen and her relatives for a short time when her father sent her off to cover Prince Charles on an early skiing holiday in the Swiss resort.

Despite Terry Fincher's strict warning not to go skiing herself, Jayne ignored his advice and the inevitable happened. 'I broke my leg in three places and had to be flown home before I had taken even one picture,' she explains. 'To make matters worse the other photographers took me in a taxi to the airport but stopped on the way at the Prince's chalet to check what he was up to. I almost cried when Charles came out of the door wearing a funny mask on his face and posed for some crazy pictures. There I was with my leg in plaster stuck in the back seat of the taxi unable to move.'

Realising that Jayne's accident was the worst break of her career the Prince sent her a letter of sympathy. She still treasures its contents so much that to this day she has never revealed what he wrote.

On the same trip an Australian television film crew arrived from London because they suspected the Prince had a girlfriend with him, and they were wondering if they could catch him with the next Queen of England.

In those days relations between the press and the Prince were so relaxed that the TV reporter simply knocked on the door of the chalet and asked for the Prince's policeman. Instead, the Prince himself opened the door and amazed to learn they were Australian said: 'Bloody hell, fancy coming all the way over here to film me.' Slightly shocked by the royal oath, the TV crew mentioned it in their filmed report and the prim Aussie reporters splashed it all over their front pages.

For some years Prince Charles was very keen on TV coverage of his activities. Television editors and producers were very circumspect and very rarely broadcast royal conversations that their microphones picked up. Their reports were much more bland and more flattering than newspaper stories often were. After some well-timed approaches by Independent

Television News Charles finally agreed to be filmed with Princess Diana for a TV special.

Although not happy about the idea of being quizzed on camera the Prince decided that this was one sure way to stop malicious gossip about his marriage.

He was particularly annoyed by an American magazine article describing his private life as a real Palace Dallas. It painted him as a Windsor wimp and his wife as a Dynasty-style super-bitch everyone loved to hate.

Another inaccurate story which irritated him was a report, first published in the United States, and later picked up by the English press. This described him as a crank who dabbled in black magic and used a Ouija board to communicate with his late great uncle Lord Mountbatten. Only on television, Charles realised, could he be seen and heard telling the world the truth behind the ridiculous rumours.

The royal scoop for ITN, called 'In Person: The Prince and Princess of Wales', was presented in October 1985 by the courtly Sir Alastair Burnet. He conducted a forty-five-minute interview with the royal couple sitting side by side on a silk sofa in the drawing room of their Kensington Palace home.

One by one Charles and Diana laughed off the ludicrous tales about their private life. Opening their hearts to the viewers they appeared as a normal, happy couple who, despite being trapped in the unrelenting glare of world attention, were determined to preserve an ordinary family life.

Upsetting the Ouija board theory, Charles declared: 'I don't even know what they are. I've never seen one.' He added: 'I'm not interested in the occult or any of these things. I'm purely interested in being open-minded.'

But anxious to defend alternative medicine, he admitted: 'I think I'm becoming more eccentric as I get older.'

Diana also seized the chance to deny rumours of a rift with Charles' sister Anne. 'I'm her biggest fan,' she insisted. 'We've always hit it off very well and I think she's marvellous.'

She then attacked the idea that she spends a vast amount of her time shopping. 'My clothes are not my priority,' she

Dazzling Melbourne with a necklace worn as a headband when her tiara got left behind in London, November 1985

Loyal wife Diana is right behind her man on a visit to Spain

Charles gets to the point during a speech in Swaziland

Diana's got the chic of Araby on a tour of Saudi Arabia, 1986

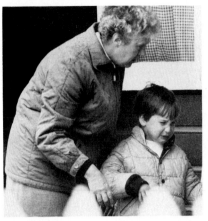
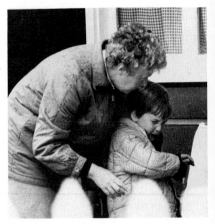
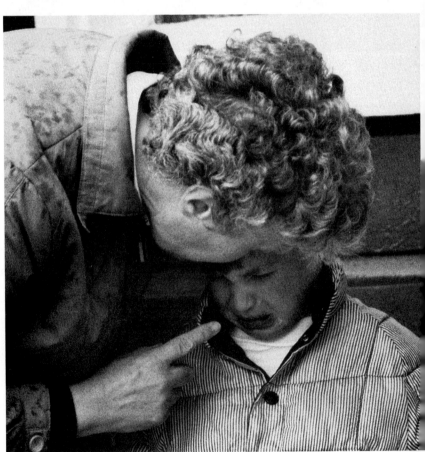

*A right royal rollocking . . . deputy nanny Olga Powell gives a tearful William
a ticking off for running on to the polo field, Windsor, 1987*

*A degree of success: the Princess accepts an Honorary Fellowship of the Royal
College of Obstetricians and Gynaecologists, June 1987*

Left: beating the drum for Britain with a Swazi princess in Africa, March 1987

Below: Charles gives Diana a pat Down Under on the last day of their first New Zealand tour

A loser at polo gets a consolation prize from his winner of a wife

Diana wanted to stay on at the French Film Festival in May 1987, but Charles said no Cannes do

declared adding that her husband liked to see her looking smart but fashion was not her passion.

Explaining that she often needed to change her clothes two or even three times a day when on tours abroad she argued that she needed a large wardrobe. 'I couldn't go around in a leopardskin,' she added with a teasing smile.

More than 21 million people watched the royal chat show in Britain and at least 200 million more saw it screened in other countries around the world. The programme was so popular that Prince Charles was persuaded to film a second documentary, 'In Private, In Public: the Prince and Princess of Wales', which was shown in Britain in September 1986.

After it was broadcast newspaper reports claimed Prince Charles found the cameras so intrusive he vowed never to repeat the experience. ITN's filmcrew shot around 400 hours of video film for the programme which lasted only two hours on the screen. When shown a preview of the show Prince Charles asked the producer to cut a sequence in which his family splashed about in the swimming pool at their country home Highgrove. As someone close to the household revealed: 'He felt it improper for the public to see the Princess quite so informally in a swimsuit. He was already annoyed about photographs taken of her wearing a brief bikini during their holiday in Majorca several weeks earlier. That is why he changed his mind and refused to allow the swimming pool scene to go out.'

A Buckingham Palace spokesman quickly denied that Prince Charles had resented the cameras following him around for so long. 'The Prince and Princess gave their fullest cooperation throughout and if they had felt there was any element of intrusiveness they would have said so.'

Privately, royal aides revealed that the Prince simply was not very impressed with the result of the entire production. 'In the end it just did not seem worth the effort involved,' explained one of them. 'The idiotic rumours about his private life did not stop. I think the Prince felt nothing was really achieved by allowing the cameras into his home.'

The ITN crew had noted that filming went smoothly whenever Diana and the small princes were involved. But tension crept into the atmosphere when Charles was called on to do his bit. 'The Princess was totally at ease in front of the cameras but her husband was uptight the whole time,' one crew member observed. 'He kept agreeing to film certain jobs then changing his mind. We were particularly disappointed when he gave us permission to film aboard Concorde when he and the Princess returned from a visit to Vienna. The next thing we heard was he didn't want us aboard. We never really found out why.'

Surprisingly, Charles approved one fascinating sequence in the film although advisers warned him he might be sorry. Wandering around his Highgrove garden he made a kooky confession. He loved to spend as much free time as possible there, he explained. 'I just come and talk to the plants, really. Very important to talk to them. They respond, I find,' he said then laughed rather sheepishly.

Next day in the popular press Charles appeared more potty than greenhouse. The Prince, who had also publicly backed trendy, alternative lifestyles such as fringe medicine, organic farming and meditation, was a true English eccentric, or so newspaper readers were led to believe. Cartoonists, comedians and television satirists picked up this light-hearted comment and turned it into a running joke. This short and simple sentence will no doubt haunt him forever.

The Prince understands that journalists are always under pressure to produce good stories and that these rarely result from the boring jobs he carries out on the royal roadshow. Yet he seems disappointed and surprised that the ultra-professional members of the Rat Pack find his private life more newsworthy than his public duties.

His marriage, his mental health and the antics of his children endlessly fascinate the British people and many millions more around the world. This obsessive interest in his family is the price the Royals pay for the popularity of the monarchy, now at an all-time high.

The Prince would perhaps feel slightly better about the microscopic scrutiny of the media if he knew that of all the

Queen's family he is the most respected by the Rat Pack. This hard-eyed group of royal watchers is not easily impressed, but the Prince of Wales is their undoubted favourite. At times he seems to return their feelings with a rather grudging regard. On his first tour of Canada he summed up the peculiar relationship he enjoys with the press in a poem. No one could put it better.

Impossible, unapproachable, God only knows,
The light's always dreadful and he won't damn-well pose.
Most maddening, most curious, he simply can't fail
It's always the same with the old Prince of Wales.

Insistent, persistent the Press never end
One day they will drive me right round the bend
Recording, rephrasing, every word that I say,
It's got to be news at the end of the day.

9

The Image of a King

Prince Charles flew into a rage when he spotted a photographer focusing his lens on him as he dug up heather on the banks of the River Dee. 'Buzz off, go on, leave me alone,' he shouted as the newsman blazed away with his Nikon motordrive camera.

The Prince was in an open place, visible from a public road that winds along the opposite bank of the river. He was enjoying one of his frequent breaks from royal duties at his grandmother's Highland home, Birkhall. Wearing chest-high waders as he prepared to go fishing he provided a tempting target for any passing cameraman. He had been photographed in virtually the same place hundreds of times in the past without protesting. In fact, two months earlier he had agreed to play with his sons on the same riverbank so that photographers could get pictures of them together. Why did he object so strongly when he was spotted rooting around in the heather?

Some might say he resented the intrusion on his free time. Others might wonder if the Prince had a guilty conscience. The visit to the riverbank was the sixth time in five months that Prince Charles had taken time off from his royal duties. Perhaps he did not want anyone to think that he was loafing.

His short break in the Highlands was a bit of luck. The June election in 1987 meant that the few official engagements the Prince had scheduled for that month had to be cancelled. He had planned to make a speech during the Royal Institute of British Architects' debate with the Londoners' Society on 20 June. But fearing some of his comments might be thought too political his appearance was dropped.

Suddenly finding himself with three days free of engagements the Prince flew up to Scotland to stay with the Queen Mother at Birkhall. His trip happened to follow the other break he had enjoyed the previous week staying with a crofter's family on the island of Berneray in the Hebrides. Reporters began to ask questions about why Charles was disappearing from London and leaving his wife behind so often. Why had he suddenly become the hermit heir?

When the Prince saw the photographer watching him from the other side of the river he blew his top. He felt he was being unfairly hounded. But was his anger totally justified? If he felt the need to run away regularly from his family, it was certainly reasonable to wonder why he did it so often. Most of the Queen's subjects feel fortunate if they can take one, or at most two, holiday breaks each year. The Prince of Wales seems to dash off to all kinds of wonderful places whenever he feels like it. Six trips in five months seems a bit excessive.

Of course, wherever he goes Prince Charles takes his job with him. Paperwork follows him around the world. He frequently works late into the night on reports, government papers and correspondence. But the public is not terribly aware of this. If his desk work ever does receive any publicity it is just a line or two of background in a story concentrating on some other aspect of his life.

If he was judged solely on what is made public the Prince of Wales could look like a rather lazy man who plays much harder than he works. As far as the man in the street can see the Prince of Wales' job involves going to various places around Britain in a limousine, waving and smiling a bit, making the odd speech at a banquet, whizzing off to tour exotic spots on the globe, and taking a lot of time off in between. It looks like a cushy number.

This is, of course, a false picture of the man. But it is usually the only picture available. His work is not very exciting so it usually gets less publicity than his leisure time. What we see most is the wealthy sportsman indulging his love of two very expensive pastimes – polo and hunting.

It costs £80,000 a year to run his string of polo ponies. Just one mount may cost anywhere from £12,000 to £25,000 and then there are stable costs, horseboxes, grooms' expenses, and equipment like saddles and other tack. A face guard to protect His Royal Handsomeness can cost as much as £74. Breeches, hand-tailored, naturally, are priced from £40 up. Leather boots are at least £170. And leather kneepads add another £40 to the total bill. And most of these need to be replaced fairly frequently. For example, polo sticks, which quite often do not survive a single game, cost around £21 each.

The Prince pays for this out of his own pocket. But it is a snob sport that only the super-rich can enjoy, and it may seem an odd choice for a man who frequently claims: 'I just want to be normal.' There is nothing very ordinary about polo. Few ordinary people can afford entrance fees to the clubs, let alone the cost of equipping themselves for a game.

Many of the other luxuries he enjoys such as cruises aboard the Royal Yacht, trips on aircraft of the Queen's Flight, and using helicopters like taxis, cost the taxpayers millions of pounds each year. A major refit for the Queen's floating palace *Britannia*, undertaken in 1987, was estimated to cost £10 million, although the final bill could be much higher. And two new BAe 146 jets which entered royal service the same year had a price tag of £33 million. This is on top of the £3 million bill to service and maintain the entire Queen's Flight.

This luxury transport is used not only by Charles and Diana but also by all the working members of the Queen's family, and occasionally some government officials. But it is often used very casually. Helicopters, in particular, are frequently used by Royals who dislike getting stuck in traffic jams like ordinary folk.

When Prince Charles goes on tours abroad he usually takes his polo manager, Major Ronald Ferguson, along too. Whenever he can he tries to squeeze a game into his work schedule. So the Major almost always goes with him to Australia and America. The host country sometimes picks up the bill for his accommodation, or he may stay at the ambassador's or Governor's residence, and there are usually one or two free seats on a royal flight. So his presence on such jaunts does not create too much extra expense.

But the cost of the Prince's pleasures is not the point. How does Charles justify this? The short answer is he doesn't. The Prince of Wales feels he doesn't have to.

He also does not think any explanation is needed for taking at least ten weeks holiday every year when most of the Queen's subjects are lucky to get three or four. Prince Charles may need such lengthy and frequent breaks from his duties if the pressures are great. But he does not seem aware that by taking such a great amount of time off without any explanation, he seems not just privileged, but work-shy.

The result is an ever widening credibility gap between the Prince and the people. Only the great affection the Queen's subjects have for her son has prevented more questions being asked about Charles' apparently self-indulgent lifestyle.

The staff of the Buckingham Palace press office are responsible for providing information about the Royal Family and safeguarding their reputations. Fortunately, they have always been very able public relations executives. But there are not enough of them to cope with the tremendous flood of inquiries that pour in from all over the world every day.

As Victor Chapman revealed a few months before he left royal service: 'The trouble is the number of staff in our office has decreased in recent years while the number of Royals we look after has doubled.'

At the time of writing there are three full-time press officers plus secretaries and clerks dealing with inquiries about more than thirty members of the Queen's family. They provide a twenty-four-hour service to the press because they frequently get calls from abroad late at night or very early in the morning.

One or other of these spokesmen is often away on an

overseas tour with one or more of the Royals, or preparing for an upcoming tour by doing a 'recce' of the job. This means the workload back at head office is spread over even fewer people.

The reason for this apparently crazy situation is money. Good staff are expensive and the Queen is a great believer in keeping costs down. But Prince Charles became aware long ago that he and his wife, in particular, needed a super PR, expert in presenting exactly the right public image for his client. Charles and Diana are the victims of more rumours and inaccurate reports than any other members of the Royal Family.

Victor Chapman, a fifty-four-year old Canadian, joined their staff in 1982 on the day Prince William was born. Following a system in which Commonwealth countries take turns in supplying top talents to staff the Buckingham Palace press office, he was recruited for a fixed term which was later extended to five years. When his secondment from the Canadian government ended the Prince found it difficult to find a replacement.

But instead of asking another Commonwealth country to fill the gap Charles realised he needed not just another diplomat but professional public relations guidance, preferably someone experienced in corporate publicity. And he decided to interview all the candidates himself. He had realised that forking out a lot of money for a top operator in the field of corporate public relations would be a small price to pay for better publicity.

It seems a lot to expect one talented PR man or even a PR firm to solve the chief problem facing Prince Charles. What is badly needed is not so much a new press officer but a change of attitude by the Prince himself. He needs to consider what sort of image he now presents to the public. If he feels beleaguered it could be his own fault.

Prince Philip was the first critic to notice that his eldest son had wound down his schedule of official duties. It began in 1984 when his workload became much lighter. It became noticeable that Princess Anne was doing roughly four times as many jobs as her brother, and the Queen and the Duke of Edinburgh had almost the same tough schedule.

Predictably, royal critic Willie Hamilton MP accused Prince Charles of being 'a royal scrounger'. Although no one takes much notice of Britain's best-known republican, many other reports gave details of the way Charles had begun to slow down.

This led to many rows between father and son and eventually a major rift. In his usual style of shouting orders as if he were on the bridge of a warship the Queen's husband told her heir bluntly: 'You are simply not pulling your weight.' Charles disagreed and refused to discuss the matter.

The Iron Duke knew that under his guidance Princess Anne had risen from the bottom of royal popularity polls back close to the top simply by working harder. He could not understand why Prince Charles could not see that he risked losing the respect and affection of his future subjects.

And the Queen's husband was worried that the next king was out of touch with the world the British people lived in. All this stuff about fringe medicine, organic farming, vegetarian diets, meditation and listening to gurus was fine for those Bohemian types. But future kings did not dabble in such daft subjects. It showed that he was too easily swayed by any new fad that came along. Charles was forgetting what *really* mattered – hanging on to the people's esteem so the family could hang on to its throne.

Feelings between the two men became so bitter than when one walked into a room the other would find an excuse to walk out.

When tackled about such stories the Palace press office insisted that the Prince of Wales worked exceedingly hard on private meetings involved with Duchy of Cornwall and Jubilee Trust business, as well as his personal interests in pet charities. But they also admitted he spent a lot of time gardening and playing polo.

It seemed that the Duke of Edinburgh was the only person who realised that how much work Charles was *seen* to do was perhaps more important than the amount he actually did.

The situation remains much the same today. What is even more worrying to many is Prince Charles does not seem to realise he has an identity crisis. In an era of high unemployment when millions of people have blighted lives because they cannot find work it seems unwise, to say the least, for the nation's future king to look like a layabout.

One solution might be to cut down on polo, the sport that costs a mint. If, as Charles claims, he desperately needs the vigorous exercise he gains playing polo, he could take up a game that is not so snooty like tennis. This would also have the bonus of allowing him more time with his wife.

The Princess loves the sport and plays regularly with girl-friends at a ritzy private club in Shepherd's Bush, west London. The entrance fee is £500 and annual membership £475 but that is a snip compared to the cost of a stableful of polo ponies.

If Charles decides he is no ace on the courts, he might prefer to try cricket, which his wife also loves. Her father had his own cricket pitch when he lived at Park House, Sandringham.

He could also make more information about his working life available to the public via the press. One top royal aide blames the Palace press office for not doing a better job. 'We are always ready to provide details of all the hard work the Prince does, but we just don't get asked,' he complained.

But while the Buckingham Palace press office remains swamped with too much work because it is understaffed, it seems futile to expect more.

Prince Charles could solve part of the problem if he changed his attitude to honest inquiries from the media. His trek into the Kalahari desert created a lot of speculation that he was disappearing into the wilderness to sit at the feet of his guru, Sir Laurens van der Post, like a latter-day hippie. This could easily have been prevented by revealing more details of what the Prince was actually doing.

When Prince Charles flew off to Botswana to begin his camping trip in the desert, officious aides drew a veil of secrecy over the entire project. It was made clear that no press reporting on the event was welcome. A few minutes after Sir Laurens van der Post boarded the royal plane a British Embassy official arrived with Prince Charles and instructed the Royal Air Force crew not to let Sir Laurens get off again. 'We don't want him talking to any journalists,' he declared – though Sir Laurens had been only too happy to talk to the press about his Kalahari adventure.

And throughout the four days that the Prince and Sir Laurens tramped through the African outback, his press officer was back in Gaborone waiting for his boss to return, so they could fly home together. His official spokesman was available to take telephoned inquiries from the press but he did not know anything worth reporting because he was not with the royal camping party.

There is always the problem of over-enthusiastic people who work for the Prince trying to do what they think he would wish them to. Buckingham Palace courtiers always err on the side of caution when it comes to revealing anything. And they often withhold information that might put the Royals in a good light because they feel the media intrudes too much on private areas of their lives.

This can often be counter-productive. When Prince Charles flew off to Italy in April 1987 and his trip was not announced in advance, pressmen who knew he planned to go somewhere for a week's holiday made inquiries and were told that after finishing his tour of Spain the Prince would 'fly north'. This could have meant he was heading home to Britain or any other spot on the map north of the Spanish border.

Later, reporters who dug into the reasons for this secrecy suspected it could be connected with a beautiful Italian Contessa Charles met while staying in Tuscany. These ideas were soon discounted but got enough publicity to give the Palace press office a huge headache.

One of the royal spokesmen said later: 'I begged the Prince's advisers to let me release information about his trip to Italy but they repeatedly refused. He had two days of official engagements before he went off sketching in Tuscany. These should not have been hushed up. But my requests got nowhere. The result was a lot of colourful speculation about him and the Contessa.'

It may be that Prince Charles' top aides have not had enough experience to deal with such delicate matters. His private secretary Sir John Riddell joined the Prince's staff in the middle of 1985, while his deputy Humphrey Mews had only been a royal employee for six months when this problem arose.

There are indications from former top members of his staff that even when his aides do offer sensible advice the Prince quite often ignores it. This is claimed to be one of the main reasons his previous private secretary Edward Adeane resigned.

Working for the Royal Family is not always the rewarding job it may seem. Many people who would be ideal advisers to the Crown cannot afford to take the drop in pay required to work for the Palace. Salaries are much lower than they could earn in the City or in industry.

Other men of the right calibre frankly cannot be bothered with all the protocol attached to royal service. There are antiquated customs like 'taking leave'. This hangover from medieval times forbids members of the Royal Household to go to bed without saying a formal goodnight to the Prince and Princess. Each person must bow or curtsey to their employers. Each morning when first sighting Charles and Diana their staff must also bow low or bend a knee and address each by the title Your Royal Highness. From then on throughout the day they use the more usual 'Sir' or 'Ma'am'.

But keeping up such traditions can be very time-consuming. On their tour of Spain the Prince and Princess were staying at the El Pardo palace about twenty miles outside Madrid. But Victor Chapman was booked with the press corps into the Palace Hotel right in the centre of the city. This meant that each night after the Prince and Princess had finished work for the day, sometimes around midnight, Victor Chapman had to drive out to the El Pardo palace just to 'take leave' of his bosses.

At the end of an exhausting day he found it a royal pain to spend an extra hour driving out of town and back again just to say goodnight. He finally asked Prince Charles if he had his permission to forget all about 'taking leave' for the duration of the tour. Realising it was a sensible suggestion, the Prince agreed.

Working for the Royal Family must often seem like stepping back into a world that vanished a hundred years ago. Despite the introduction of computers at Buckingham Palace the administration has changed very little throughout the last few reigns.

Royal aides can only make suggestions or recommendations. The boss has the final word. And sometimes advice from staff is overlooked when a conflicting suggestion comes from another respected source. More and more often these days when Prince Charles comes up with a controversial speech he has been heavily influenced by one or other of his unofficial advisers.

These men of maturity and wisdom are like father figures and to a certain extent have filled the gap left by Lord Mountbatten. They include not just Sir Laurens van der Post but Dr Armand Hammer, the American oil mogul, Lord Tonypandy, the former Speaker of the House of Commons and, occasionally, the architect Rod Hackney.

This distinguished group, who have been frequently asked to join small select parties around Charles and Diana's dinner table, are all well-meaning people who share the Prince's desire to leave the world a better place than they found it. But their main considerations are not necessarily those of the monarchy.

Sir Laurens, using his experiences in the African bush and as a prisoner of the Japanese during World War II, has helped the Prince gain the spiritual serenity to cope with his demanding role.

Lord Tonypandy, a deeply religious Welshman, keeps the Prince in touch with general developments in the world of national politics. And Charles gets a global view of political change from his old friend Dr Armand Hammer. The founder of Occidental Petroleum has been doing deals with the Russians and the Americans for more than forty years and has a tremendous insight into the workings of the superpowers. And he is always ready to dip into his seemingly bottomless pockets to fund Charles' pet projects from the raising of the *Mary Rose* to the United World Colleges. A good indication of his closeness to Prince Charles was the fact that the elderly American was the first visitor to Kensington Palace after the royal couple brought their first baby home from hospital.

Conservation is one of the Prince's passions and he is advised on all aspects of it by scientist and writer Dr Miriam Rothschild. And it was his concern about the problems created by the decay of inner cities which brought Charles into contact with Dr Rod Hackney, the Macclesfield architect who later rose to become President of the Royal Institute of British Architects.

It is the direct result of his friendship with these experts that the Prince has begun to attack what he believes is wrong with modern society.

But his idealism is often tinged with naivety. Inspired no doubt by talks with one or other of his grey-haired gurus he made a speech in October 1986 accusing builders of allowing inner cities to fester while gobbling up huge sections of the countryside.

He provoked a storm when he told the National House-builders Conference in London that the results were an ever increasing spiral of decay, poor physical and mental health and general low morale.

Top building firms immediately pointed out that they did not redevelop inner city sites because of problems with councils refusing to release them. They also explained that most house-hunters did not look for property in rundown city areas when they could buy much more desirable homes on greenfield sites.

Lord Northfield, head of one building consortium, claimed angrily that Prince Charles had been 'hijacked by the loony Green brigade'. This led to rumbles in right-wing political circles that the future king was far too easily influenced by people with eccentric views. One senior Cabinet Minister said: 'Prince Charles has every right to speak out on issues but he needs a back-up team to do his research and help him write his speeches to make sure that what he says is accurate.' A few weeks later the Prince apologised at another conference and practically admitted he had made a gaffe.

The general belief was that the Prince had good intentions but got carried away by his own enthusiasm and did not know enough about his subject. The Prince of Wales had fallen into his credibility gap once again.

It wasn't the first time Charles had spoken out about something close to his heart and infuriated a lot of other people. In 1978 the Vatican launched an amazing attack on him when he seemed critical of the Pope for refusing Prince Michael permission to marry his divorced bride, Marie Christine von Reibnitz, in church.

But some of his suggestions are welcomed. When he urged big businesses to give at least one per cent of their profits to fund projects to help small, struggling industries, he was congratulated.

He believes such cash gifts will create new small firms and will help to reduce unemployment. Appealing to the better nature of businessmen, he asked them to buy locally from small companies and pay their bills promptly. He also suggested they could offer unused premises to local enter- prises for peppercorn rents, and lend key personnel so their expertise can help new companies to start up.

The Confederation of British Industries welcomed the Prince's plan. Mr Simon Carruth, secretary of its small firms council, said: 'We agree with the moral pressure Prince Charles is exerting.'

Such worthy work gets little publicity, however, and the idea lingers that Prince Charles is a woolly-minded do-gooder.

He seems convinced that both his work and his private life are misrepresented by the media. The depth of his feeling was revealed by an equerry who spoke to a reporter from the Press Association in May 1987. He said the Prince was dismayed about the type of publicity he was getting. He was particularly upset about reports of his trip to the Hebridean island as another 'Charles going off alone again to find himself' story.

The equerry told the reporter: 'There are lots of people living many different lifestyles in Britain. One day he is going to be king and before then he wants to find out how his future subjects really live – to see life through their eyes.'

It may appear more than a coincidence that whenever the Prince goes off on these educational trips he does not spend a week working down a mine or join the dustmen emptying rubbish bins. He always chooses a rather pleasant place to work. It would be truly wonderful if all the workers in Britain had such pleasant conditions.

Prince Charles fails to see that people would be far more impressed by his sincerity if he took on a lousy job like working on a factory conveyor belt or spent a week caring for the mentally handicapped. He would gain a far better under-standing of what life is like for most of the Queen's subjects than planting potatoes or fishing for his lunch in the Hebrides. Not many people would consider his odd jobs for the crofter on Berneray hard work. How can the Prince reasonably expect to get fairer treatment from the press if he fails to understand this?

This so-called unfair treatment is exacerbated by the lack of access given to the reporters and photographers who relay his activities to the outside world. When the Prince and Princess meet accredited pressmen at the start of every overseas tour they shake hands and spend between thirty seconds and a minute or two making small talk with each journalist at a press reception which lasts around forty-five minutes. The idea is to maintain friendly relations between the Palace and the press.

But similar get-togethers are never held on home ground. And no serious discussions are ever allowed to happen overseas in the short time allowed each journalist.

The Prince would probably consider that it is pointless to give more time to some newsmen who, he believes, are interested more in sensational stories than the truth. What he fails to grasp is these wild reports would never be published if reporters had better informed press officers at the Palace to brief them.

For many years most journalists took what Buckingham

Palace officials told them with a pinch of salt. This was a result of official denials that Princess Anne would announce her engagement to Captain Mark Phillips. Only days after a Palace spokesman told Fleet Street reporters that there was no serious romance the Queen released the news of her only daughter's betrothal.

This and similar incidents destroyed the credibility of the Palace press office for many years. Even if the staff did not deliberately try to misinform the press there were still times when they were kept in the dark themselves and therefore could not tell the truth.

If the Queen and Prince Charles insist on hamstringing their spokesmen by not letting them know much of what is going on they must expect the press to make mistakes sometimes.

But journalists are not totally to blame for Prince Charles' unrealistic image. In December 1986 a daily paper published a series of photographs of Prince Charles on a pheasant shoot. They were very little different from pictures taken more than fifty years ago of his grandfather and great uncles. Dressed in plus-fours and cap with his rifle under his arm Charles was shown wringing the necks of wounded birds. While gamekeepers and gundogs stood around, the Prince calmly and efficiently killed the struggling pheasants. The picture revealed another side of the compassionate Prince who visits down-and-outs. Here was a rich man enjoying his privileges just as the men in his privileged family have always done.

In one picture he was seen spinning a bird around in the air to break its neck. The Prince thought he was shielded from the public's gaze by dense woodland on the Sandringham estate. He was out for a day's shooting with King Juan Carlos of Spain and ex-King Constantine of Greece on the Norfolk estate. The royal get-together was Charles' idea to return the hospitality he had enjoyed from his friends.

What surprised many beaters that day was the arrival of four-year-old Prince William with his mother to have lunch with the men. Richard Course, executive director of the League Against Cruel Sports, said: 'It's unbelievable. They don't give a damn about public opinion.'

Charles' rough treatment of the birds was defended by sports-men who claimed he was only putting the creatures out of their misery. That would be considered a kindness if only he had not shot the birds and injured them in the first place.

The Prince has made it plain that he wants his sons to learn to shoot as soon as they are old enough to understand how to handle a gun. So the royal row with animal lovers seems sure to continue.

What made these pictures even more extraordinary to staff at Sandringham was that they had seen the Prince save the life of another half-dead bird. While sketching on the beach at Holkham during that same winter Charles came across a seagull totally soaked in oil which had obviously leaked from a tanker in the North Sea. He asked one of his gamekeepers to take care of the bird and deliver it to the nearest bird sanctuary. Aware that his staff might decide the bird was too far gone and put it out of its misery when his back was turned the soft-hearted Prince added: 'Now I want to hear how this bird gets on. Let me know when it's well enough to be set free. I am patron of a bird protection society, you know.'

He does not appear to be aware of the contradictions in his behaviour. He wants to do as he likes then wonders why people criticise him for it. He says he just wants to be 'ordinary' but he would not consider giving up his ritzy lifestyle. He drops out whenever he feels like it then can't understand if people think this is odd.

Another problem is his notorious inability to be decisive. He never really knows what he wants. This was forcibly brought home to me by the Prince when we met up after he had been to Africa. 'You know I never read the newspapers,' he said, 'but I read the story you wrote about me shopping in Nairobi. I didn't like it at all. You said I was no good at shopping.'

He was referring to a light-hearted piece about his visit to a fruit and vegetable market where the natives thought the Royal bwana was bananas. It was obvious he hadn't a clue how Diana does the housekeeping at home.

The Prince, who loves gardening and grows vegetables to

give to his friends as gifts, mixed up cabbages with carrots, avocados with mangos and didn't even know his onions. He pointed to some green onions and asked: 'What are these?' Next he tried the tomatoes and sniffed one instead of feeling it to see if it was fresh.

The jokey story went on to describe how every time he made a comment about the produce he made a blunder.

In the middle of complaining about all this, Prince Charles suddenly admitted: 'Actually, you're right, you know. I am no good at shopping. You see I can never make up my mind. It takes me ages to decide on anything. I find it very difficult. My wife is exactly the opposite – she always knows just what she wants.'

Princess Diana has decided that she wants a more serious image and has done something about it. Dynasty Di is now being transformed into Diana the Do-gooder.

Meanwhile, her husband sits around with a fishing rod in his hand or goes sketching foreign scenery in between dashing off to the polo grounds. And he wonders why some people think this is odd.

10

The Shadow on the Throne

The day Princess Diana faced a killer still makes the officers of Scotland Yard's Royal Protection Squad shudder. The Princess's bodyguard, Inspector Allan Peters, had only a split second to decide whether to draw his pistol and fire or try to avoid trouble by pushing her out of the way.

As his hand hovered over his holster he shouted: 'Get out of the way!' to get a clear line of fire across the packed room. Then he roughly grabbed the Princess by the arm and ordered: 'C'mon, we're getting out of here.'

Princess Diana was visiting the Broadwater Farm Estate in Tottenham, north London, in February 1985, when her police officer spotted a sinister figure in the crowd. It was Winston Silcott, the gang leader later convicted of hacking to death P.C. Keith Blakelock in the Broadwater riot trial and jailed for thirty years.

The cool, sure way Inspector Peters handled a potentially lethal situation is now described to Scotland Yard's trainee officers as an example of how to cope with a royal crisis.

When Diana's visit to the grim pile of concrete tower blocks was planned tension was running high on the estate. Only months later it became the scene of the horrific riot during which the unarmed police constable was butchered.

As usual the Royal Protection Squad officer guarding the Princess tried to check out the estate before she arrived. But local Tottenham police warned him that a 'recce', as it is known, was impossible. 'Even our officers are not allowed into the place without first getting an OK from community leaders,' they warned, adding: 'This is a no-go area. You must understand that a riot could break out here any minute. The whole place is a powder keg about to explode.'

When the Princess arrived at the estate, Inspector Peters and his back-up officer Sergeant Steve Skinner sensed that trouble was in the air. They had been thoroughly briefed about Broadwater Farm and the bad feeling among the residents directed at local police.

When they escorted Diana into the Broadwater community centre thirty or forty youths were playing snooker and pool. Their worst fears were confirmed when the Tottenham police superintendent pointed out a tall, dark, threatening figure at the back of the room.

'That's Winston Silcott, the most dangerous man on this patch,' he warned. 'We have been following him for weeks in connection with a case involving the murder of a young boxer. But we lost him when he entered the estate because we didn't dare go in after him – there would have been a riot.' The police chief added: 'I'd love to know what he is doing here. Don't take your eyes off him for a second. He's crazy. He could do anything.'

Winston Emanuel Silcott, then a twenty-four-year-old greengrocer, had a criminal career that began in January 1977 when he was charged with burglary and theft but was later given a conditional discharge. He was in and out of Borstals in the next few years after more burglary charges and charges of receiving stolen goods.

But from theft he turned to violence. In 1979 he was arrested for malicious wounding after a dance hall stabbing. The following year Leonard McIntosh, a young musician, died at a West Indian blues party in Wood Green, north London. Silcott was suspected of involvement but he was acquitted of murder at a retrial after an earlier jury failed to reach a verdict.

A police driver was also stabbed in August 1983 when loading prisoners into a van. Silcott was standing nearest to him but there was insufficient evidence to make any charge stick.

Then in December 1984, three months before Princess Diana arrived at Broadwater Farm, a young boxer called Tony Smith was killed at another blues party. (Silcott was eventually convicted of his murder and sentenced to thirty years in prison.)

When Allan Peters first noticed the man whom the police had been tracking he saw a threatening figure. The six-foot two-inch killer was wearing a black balaclava which hid a bushy beard and most of his features. Only his dark eyes, glaring at the Princess, could be seen as he loomed up at the back of the crowd.

As Diana moved through the crowd she turned in Silcott's direction. At that moment he bent over a snooker table, and with a thunderous crack that echoed around the room his cue sent the coloured balls ricocheting all over the green baize. To the anxious police officers surrounding the Princess it had the same shattering effect as a gunshot.

Royal bodyguards recall that Allan Peters later told them how desperate he felt as the future Queen of England entrusted to his care came face to face with a suspected killer.

Peters was alone with his back-up man because he was not allowed to take more officers into the estate. A heavy police presence was forbidden, in keeping with the local police's low-profile policy. As he told his colleagues later: 'I was trying to keep one eye on Silcott and the other on the crowd of youths who were shuffling closer and closer to the Princess. They were young and fit and I knew whose side they would be on if trouble broke out.

'But what horrified me most was that if I had to go for my gun I had no clear line of fire. I knew Silcott had nothing to lose by killing her. He was certain to get life if convicted of murdering the young boxer, but by assassinating the Princess of Wales he would be guaranteed a page in history. I knew the man was dangerous and I suspected he could be armed as well. As he edged closer through the crowd I knew I had to stop him.'

Peters was also concerned that if he did draw his revolver anyone who got in the way might be hit if a gun battle broke out. But most of all he was determined to shield Diana from Silcott at any cost. With a whispered command, he ordered his back-up officer to move ahead and block Silcott's path to the Princess.

Peters, a blond, blue-eyed mountain of a man who is six foot four inches tall and weighs a hefty seventeen stone, is so fiercely protective and loyal that Diana is known to be totally relaxed whenever he is by her side. Oblivious to the killer in the crowd and the terrifying atmosphere in the room, she chatted cheerfully with the unemployed youngsters who gathered around.

One of the first requirements of an officer protecting the Royal Family is he must not be a trigger-happy Billy the Kid. Allan Peters was well aware that guns had been drawn very rarely by Royal Protection Squad officers. When he discusses the incident now with junior officers he tells them: 'The one good thing about guarding a woman is that if the worst happens, you can pick her up and run for it. I thought I'd have to do that if Silcott came any closer. I was quite prepared to throw the Princess over my shoulder and make a dash for the door.' He admits that if necessary he was also ready to draw his revolver and assume the hands-around-the-gun-butt firing position.

Ron Bell, the Press Association's veteran royal photographer, remembers the desperate way Peters reacted. He heard the normally quiet officer scream at him: 'Get out of the way!' Peters then grabbed the Princess and shoved her quickly outside to her waiting car. But he did not relax his guard until he had his royal charge safely back inside the walls of Kensington Palace. It was then that he told the shocked Princess about the suspected killer who had come so close to her.

Inspector Peters' vigilance and rapid reaction to an explosive situation had protected her from any fear. And from then on Diana has relied even more on his guidance whenever he escorts her.

An indication of the trust between them came soon afterwards in the ITN documentary about the Prince and Princess of

Wales. Diana reminded Charles that on their flight home from a tour of the United States Allan Peters would celebrate his birthday. 'We must make sure he has a good time,' she added.

Inspector Peters' colleagues also congratulated him on his expert handling of a tough job. They recalled that the only time anyone could remember a Royal Protection Squad police officer drawing a weapon and using it was during the attempted kidnap of Princess Anne in 1974.

Peters himself had threatened to use his revolver once before while accompanying Princess Diana and the Duchess of York on a skiing holiday. When a particularly persistent member of the German paparazzi followed them Peters had warned him to leave them alone, but the German had a vicious dog on a leash and threatened to set the animal on the policeman. Peters assured him that if he did that, he would gun it down as soon as it moved. Convinced that he meant it the photographer gave up chasing his quarry.

A more bizarre instance of a gun being drawn in anger occurred some years earlier and involved Chief Inspector John MacLean, who was Prince Charles' bodyguard. On a trip abroad with the Prince he was sharing a hotel room with Charles' aide Francis Cornish. As the royal official later explained, he was sound asleep in the middle of the night when he was woken by a sudden noise. As he struggled awake through a fog of sleep he suddenly saw the naked figure of MacLean in classic feet apart firing position with his gun pointed straight at Cornish's head. Several heart-stopping seconds elapsed before he managed to make the policeman realise he posed no threat.

It later turned out that the sound which had suddenly roused MacLean must have come from somewhere outside the room, but psyched up to react instinctively, the police inspector had leapt out of bed and snatched up his revolver without a pause to think what he was doing and pointed it at the first moving object he focused on.

MacLean always declared that he was ready to lay down his life if necessary to protect the heir to the throne. Then he would add jokingly: 'But if anything does happen to him, I hope it happens on my day off.'

The Royal Protection Squad is a superb team of SAS-trained police officers hand-picked to guard the Queen and her closest relatives. They are selected from the best and brightest men and women in the Metropolitan Police Force and renowned for their supremely fast reactions.

Apart from the usual skills of a top cop each needs a thorough grounding in etiquette and protocol. As they work in such close proximity to the Royal Family, guarding them day and night, they must be totally discreet and trustworthy. Officers who pass these stringent tests must also have completely clean records as even the most minor offence could disqualify them.

The Squad is now headed by Deputy Assistant Commissioner John Cracknell and his number two, Chief Inspector J. C. Strachan, and the efficiency and loyalty of the officers who serve under them are unquestioned.

The closest they have come to losing a member of the family was during the attempt to kidnap Princess Anne in 1974. The Queen's only daughter and her husband, Captain Mark Phillips, were driving along the Mall back to Buckingham Palace from an evening engagement when a Ford Escort – driven by a man called Ian Ball – overtook their car and forced it into the kerb.

The would-be kidnapper leapt out of his car and fired a gun into the rear window of the royal limousine. Then he ordered the Princess to get out. When she refused he tried to drag her out of the car, but Captain Phillips held on firmly to his wife and managed to keep her inside. Princess Anne's bodyguard Sergeant Jim Beaton repeatedly tried to tackle Ball but each time he was shot – first in the chest, then in the hand and finally in the stomach. Royal chauffeur Alexander Callendar, who disobeyed the gunman's order to stay behind the wheel, was wounded in the chest.

A young policeman on duty across the road at St James's Palace rushed over to lend assistance and was also gunned down. Two passers-by also tried to help and received serious bullet wounds. Squads of police alerted by the gunfire rushed to the scene and arrested Ian Ball. A ransom note demanding £3 million for the safe return of the Princess Royal was found in his possession.

Princess Anne, along with her husband and her lady-in-waiting, Rowena Brassey, was miraculously unhurt. The next day she visited the five victims of the shooting as they recovered in hospital and later they all received medals for their bravery. But everyone realised that the story might have had a much more tragic ending.

Ian Ball eventually appeared in court, pleaded guilty and was ordered to be detained indefinitely under the Mental Health Act in a special hospital. His attack was the work of a lone madman and no deep, dark plots were suspected.

However, both police and Royals believe there is no way anyone can be protected from this sort of dedicated assassin or lunatic who cares nothing for his own safety. An incident in New Zealand in which an egg was thrown at the Queen in 1986 gave security chiefs a grim reminder of this. 'Some crazy person might get one of the Royal Family but we'll definitely get him,' one of the Squad said at the time. 'To be certain of killing one of the family a murderer would have to get very close. And in that case he would never get away. We can promise you that.'

Princess Anne, with the benefit of her chilling experience, faces up to the dangers of her position. In a BBC TV interview with the Archbishop of Canterbury's envoy Terry Waite, who was kidnapped in Beirut a few months later, the Princess said royal duties must always come before fears for her own safety. 'If someone decides that it's worth their while either kidnapping or killing you – then I don't think there's anything constructive we or anybody else can do about it.'

The Princess has survived more than one attempt on her life. As she spoke, a plan to take her hostage while she was in Brazil only weeks earlier was still fresh in her mind. A gang of criminals had decided to kidnap Anne and hold her in exchange for the release of their leader, a notorious cocaine dealer, who was in prison. Fortunately, this wild scheme was foiled by the Brazilian authorities.

She said that although she was constantly aware of her vulnerability she always tried to push such thoughts to the back of her mind. 'If it's there all the time you become unconscious of it. Threats are nothing else, and in some ways it's very difficult to take them seriously,' she added. 'It's something that when things are going well people tend to forget about. But that makes it more dramatic when it happens again.' The Princess told Terry Waite that she was not worried by the bungled attempt to kidnap her in the Mall. 'He was on his own. That made it slightly easier,' she explained. 'If he had brought a friend it might have been more difficult.'

Her narrow escape emphasises the risks the Royal Family encounter every day of their lives. But once her assailant had been jailed the incident was forgotten by most people, though security continued to be tight but never obvious.

But after the assassination of Lord Mountbatten by the IRA in 1979 everything changed. It was widely believed until then, although never by the police, that terrorists would never actually attack the Royal Family as such an attack would shock even the terrorists' own supporters. Then 'Uncle Dickie' was killed by a horrific blast from fifty pounds of explosives planted on board his fishing boat in Co. Sligo. He had been on holiday with his family in Ireland, and they had just set off on a trip across the bay near his home Classiebawn Castle when their boat was blown to pieces. Three other people died as a result of the insane attack.

Prince Charles seemed at the time more affected by the tragedy than anyone else in his family. Staff reported later that he was absolutely distraught – not only by the senseless death of the man he called his Honorary Grandfather but also by the slaughter of his fourteen-year-old godson Nicholas Brabourne.

The Prince was on holiday in Iceland when he learned the shocking news, and he flew back to London immediately hoping to find some way to help. He wanted to rush straight over to Ireland where Lord Mountbatten's grandson and heir Norton Knatchbull, now Lord Romsey, had taken charge. In despair the grieving Prince told his staff: 'I just wish I could put an Army uniform on and get over there and get the bastards who did this.'

But royal advisers would not consider allowing the Prince to go anywhere near the danger zone. His office pointed out that his presence in the vicinity of the assassination would create tremendous security problems. Charles was forced to give in, complaining: 'I feel so helpless.'

Prince Charles himself had for some years lived with the threat of an attack; he knew his name was and might still be on an IRA hit list. But he was totally unprepared for the murder of his young godson Nicholas, and the family's teenage boatman. 'What a waste of young lives,' he repeated over and over again. Neither could he understand why the Dowager Lady Brabourne, the eighty-year-old mother of Lord Mountbatten's son-in-law, should also die in the explosion.

The IRA attack forced all the Royals to confront the unthinkable. Any one of them could be sacrificed at any time to any crazy cause. The Prince decided to issue instructions that if terrorists ever succeeded in snatching him he did not wish to be ransomed. 'I don't want to die, but I don't want anyone to pay a ransom either,' he explained.

Three years later the shadow of fear hung over the family again. Early one summer morning in June 1982 a deranged man called Michael Fagan dodged Buckingham Palace's security cordons to enter the Royal Apartments. Shortly before 7.15 a.m. he walked into an ante-chamber leading to the Queen's bedroom. Here he smashed a glass ashtray and, dripping blood from a cut thumb, he calmly entered the sleeping Queen's room.

It was only when he dragged open the curtains that the woman he wanted to see sat up in bed wondering who had disturbed her. As the Queen later told detectives, she realised at once that the intruder was not a servant because he opened the curtains by hand instead of using the pull-cord.

Terrified, but trying hard not to show it, the Queen ordered the stranger to get out but he just ignored her. Next, she tried to get help. But a series of police blunders prevented anyone rushing to her rescue. No one came when she pressed the night alarm bell by her bed. At the very first opportunity she lifted the telephone receiver, called the switchboard and said in a very normal voice that she wanted a policeman. The operator called the police lodge in the Palace precincts but six more minutes passed and still no one came.

The Queen called the switchboard again and calmly asked why no one had answered her previous call. Fortunately, Fagan then asked for some cigarettes and the Queen, who does not smoke, explained she had none in her room. This gave her an excuse to walk out of the bedroom and call for a chambermaid, Elizabeth Andrews. As soon as she saw the stranger in the room the maid immediately realised something was wrong. 'Bloody 'ell, Ma'am, what's he doing here?' she gasped.

With Elizabeth Andrews, the Queen and Michael Fagan went searching for cigarettes in the pantry down the hall. Once there a footman, Paul Wybrew, grabbed Fagan and handed him over to the police who arrived shortly afterwards. More than fifteen minutes had elapsed since the intruder had strolled into the Queen's bedroom.

As the Queen recovered from the shock she got annoyed by reports that the Duke of Edinburgh had not been sleeping in his wife's bedroom. Stories circulated that they had always had separate bedrooms, and the Queen was furious because these reports implied that she and her husband no longer had a happy and intimate relationship. In fact, only very few members of her staff knew that normally the Duke was with his wife. The Duke's valet considers himself to be the luckiest man on the royal staff because he never has to get up at an ungodly hour to wake his boss. The Duke uses an ordinary alarm because any servant trying to wake him up would embarrass his wife sleeping by his side.

Fagan's intrusion resulted in a big shake-up in security

procedures after a Scotland Yard investigation into the Queen's ordeal, but the Royal Family were still left with the feeling that Buckingham Palace was not a happy place to live. And until 1987 the Queen had always felt more secure in the country. But a frightening incident at Sandringham made her realise that safety cannot really be guaranteed anywhere.

As she was looking out of an upstairs window at Sandringham House one winter afternoon the Queen noticed a stranger darting erratically across the lawn towards her home. She pressed an alarm bell but was afraid that the intruder would burst in through the unlocked doors of the building before police could race to the rescue. Dashing quickly downstairs she ran to the front door and bolted it to keep the madman from reaching her. Then, as she peered out of a window trying to spot the man she saw an armed policeman bring him down with a rugby tackle just five feet from the door.

The Queen Mother, who had heard the commotion, walked into the room asking what was wrong. Her daughter briefly explained and together the two women watched the policeman grappling with the lunatic. Other officers arrived on the scene within a few minutes and had to restrain the struggling man with handcuffs. He began shouting obscenities as they dragged him away for questioning.

The man had got into the grounds of the Norfolk estate by scaling the Jubilee Gates at the main entrance. An alarm went off but the video surveillance system, designed to 'seek and find' intruders, somehow failed. And police, rushing from their lodge on the estate, had no idea where to look for their quarry. One quick-thinking officer, a former Guardsman, realised the best way to guard the Queen was to make for the house's front door. It was there he spotted the intruder and grabbed him in the nick of time.

When questioned later the man claimed he just wanted to see the Queen to 'cheer her up'. He was detained in a psychiatric hospital in Norwich under the Mental Health Act. Not long afterwards he was transferred to another unit in London and certified as unsafe to be released.

But the fact that he had been able to head straight for the front door unchallenged indicated that the security system at Sandringham was far from perfect. Only eight policemen were assigned to guard the ninety acres of thickly wooded grounds when the Royal Family were in residence in the belief that the electronic surveillance equipment afforded the best protection. But once again the so-called foolproof methods of protecting the Royal Family had failed, although Norfolk police claimed they were satisfied with the arrangements devised to protect the Sandringham estate.

Unlike Windsor Castle and Buckingham Palace, which are more like national monuments, the Queen had always regarded Sandringham as her retreat from the royal roundabout. For this reason she had tried to gain more privacy by limiting the number of police patrolling the property. But the number of serious incidents over the past twenty years has made every member of the family realise how terribly vulnerable they are.

This constant fear adds even more stress to people who are already under considerable pressure from their public roles. Knowing that at any moment death could come from some unexpected quarter is a horrifying prospect. For Charles, Diana and their entire family it has become a sad fact of life.

Proof that security chiefs now seriously view the possibility of an attack on a member of the Queen's family came when the Royals were ordered to undertake secret training by crack SAS troops. Prince Charles, Princess Diana, Princess Anne, the Duke and Duchess of York have all been taught the latest techniques in dealing with would-be assassins. This training, normally reserved for the élite SAS commandos, includes basic unarmed combat techniques, as well as how to reverse a car at high speed from an ambush. This expert tuition was given during secret visits by each of the Queen's relatives to the headquarters of the SAS at Hereford.

So, although intruders have broken into the grounds of Kensington Palace they have never yet entered the private apartment of the Prince and Princess of Wales. But if they do Charles and Diana will be ready for them.

Fears of such scares never completely vanish despite the best precautions. And their police protectors are never able to relax their guard. For Charles and Diana the problem of raising their children without allowing them to become prisoners of fear is one more difficulty they must face. The royal children still go out to play in London parks but they are permanently guarded by the fittest men in the Force.

When the family travel abroad they risk danger from other terrorist groups looking for a way to attract publicity for their cause. A major security operation was arranged when the royal couple took their children to Majorca for their first seaside holiday in August 1986. The Basque separatist group ETA had threatened a new wave of attacks throughout Spain at that time.

When he returned on an official tour of Spain the following year local journalists asked Prince Charles if he was still worried about attacks by ETA.

'I don't really know if I am a target,' the Prince replied explaining that he was not really disturbed about threats from ETA. 'If I were attacked it is more likely to be the IRA.' Then he added quietly: 'If your name is on the bullet there is nothing you can do about it.'

11

The Fall of the House of Windsor

Throughout her long reign Elizabeth II has never been able to shake off one ever present fear. Her uncle's abdication has always lurked in the background like a spectre reminding the Royal Family that disaster is never very far away.

When Edward VIII announced to a breathless nation that he would give up his crown to marry a divorced woman the Queen was an impressionable ten years old. Many leading members of the Establishment doubted that her father, the shy, stammering Duke of York, who was next in line of succession, was worthy to step into the breach and the country was plunged into a constitutional crisis. It was the nearest the throne had ever come to toppling.

The entire mess might have been even more catastrophic if the Fleet Street press had not reverently refused to publish reports of the romance between the King and Mrs Simpson. Although American and European newspapers had been full of stories about Edward VIII's scandalous affair for months the British people were the last to know about it. A conspiracy of silence protected the Royal Family from facing a public outcry until the last act of the tragedy was played out in the open.

This can never happen again. The Queen is very much aware that cover-ups of royal indiscretions are virtually impossible now that every member of the Royal Family lives under the searing spotlight of media attention. Even if the lowliest member of the clan were to make a slip they would all be compromised. The British people would feel entitled to ask how a family which is so privileged and is supposed to be an example to us all could permit such behaviour.

The Queen has devoted her life to repairing the damage sustained during the abdication, yet over the past thirty-five years a series of scandals has shaken the Palace to its foundations. Each one has eroded a little more of the solid base on which the Royal Family has stood for more than 150 years.

The first crisis broke around the inexperienced head of the young Queen soon after her Coronation. Her sister Princess Margaret had fallen in love with a royal equerry, Group Captain Peter Townsend, and wanted to marry him.

But the dashing war hero Townsend had been the innocent party in a divorce and horrified courtiers and politicians bitterly opposed her plans. In 1953 – when the Townsend affair became public knowledge – the climate of opinion was such that divorced people were not even permitted to enter the Royal Enclosure at Ascot. How then could such a man become the Queen's brother-in-law? The old guard at the Palace, traumatised by the abdication, would not consider changing the rules. Nothing must ever be allowed to endanger the public's respect for the Crown, they argued. The unhappy Margaret was in the same position as her uncle had been in 1939. It was a straight choice between duty and personal happiness. It was stressed that if the Princess followed her heart she would 'irreparably damage the standing of the Crown'. Her sister was head of the established Church of England which did not sanctify the remarriage of divorced persons.

Townsend was an outsider who lacked the typical courtier's aristocratic background. A civil servant's son with no private income, he had gained his job as equerry to the late King George VI on his outstanding war record. When he became a royal favourite with the whole family more senior advisers to the monarch resented his rapid rise.

A good deal of the opposition to his marriage to Margaret was as much the result of snobbery as anything else. He was a man of the world, sixteen years older than the innocent

Princess, and therefore – in some people's eyes – a cad and a bounder. He should never have overstepped the line between friendship and familiarity, according to his enemies at Court. String-pulling behind the scenes soon had the the government joining the forces against the lovers.

The old abdication arguments were dragged out to persuade the Queen that she could never condone such a marriage. Beaten into submission by threats that she would become a penniless exile from her homeland if she deserted her duty, Princess Margaret gave up the man she loved.

In retrospect it is doubtful that the British people would have been outraged by a match between a divorced man and a Princess who was then fourth in line to the throne. Margaret was never likely to have become Queen. Both she and Townsend, like the Queen herself, were ill-advised and the entire affair was totally mismanaged from the start. The lesson to be learned from the whole sad episode was not so much that a family scandal could damage the monarchy, but that incompetent royal advisers could turn it into a Palace-quaking crisis.

Princess Margaret was understandably bitter ever afterwards. Her sense of betrayal probably influenced her decision to find happiness anywhere she could from then on. But her sacrifice was long forgotten when a second storm broke around her head in 1976. The Princess had been unhappily married for many years to royal photographer Lord Snowdon when she went flying off to an island in the sun with a gardener-turned-pop-singer. The blaze of publicity surrounding her relationship with Roddy Llewellyn, who was seventeen years younger, led to the break-up of her marriage.

Questions were raised in the House of Commons about the taxpayers subsidising her luxury trip to a paradise island while the people at home were being asked to tighten their belts. Critics counted the cost of keeping this wayward Princess on the Civil List, then £55,000 a year, while money was urgently needed to save hospitals from closure.

In an attempt to stem the tide of republican outrage her estranged husband was guaranteed access to their two children and a large financial settlement if he remained silent about the break-up. Margaret's popularity with the public sank to an all-time low. It was not for another ten years, when the lonely Princess had a serious lung operation, that she again became the subject of genuine public sympathy and concern.

Meanwhile, her role as the Royal Sourpuss had been filled by the Queen's only daughter. 'I was never a fairytale Princess,' Anne quite rightly declared once when interviewed about her prickly image. For years she was dogged by reports that her marriage to the former Army captain, Mark Phillips, was heading for the rocks.

But a shockwave hit the Palace in 1981 after revelations about her friendship with her police bodyguard, a lowly sergeant. Princess Anne's former Scotland Yard minder, Peter Cross, published details of their astonishing relationship in a Sunday newspaper, describing a year of secret rendezvous with Anne after he left her service; he had been removed from Anne's side for being 'over-familiar'.

This headline-hitting drama hardly improved Anne's low rating on royal popularity polls. But she ignored the scandalous publicity while the Palace maintained a disdainful attitude and issued no comment at all. Eventually the furore died away.

The following year it was her brother Andrew's turn to cause shock and dismay. He had returned home from the Falklands conflict a war hero with the world at his feet. Only weeks later he had everyone at his throat when he flew off on holiday with a soft porn starlet posing as his wife.

For many months it seemed that the Prince was determined to marry his showgirl despite the juicy details of Koo Stark's past being splashed all over the newspapers. Still photographs from lurid scenes in her sexploitation films went around the world – the general view was that the Prince might want to make her a Princess but she was certainly no lady. And the nation wondered how the Queen could entertain such a sensational young woman as her Balmoral house guest.

This potentially explosive affair was handled with customary firmness by the powers-that-be at Court. Fearful that if they opposed the match the lovers might elope, royal advisers seemed willing to help. They cleverly suggested that the way to win public approval for the romance was to create a more respectable image for Miss Stark. She was encouraged to leave England and spend some months abroad. During this time she did a television interview in Australia, with royal backing, which was designed to show her in an attractive light as a hard-working, serious actress.

Meanwhile, Andrew sailed away to the south seas with his ship and the couple were parted for many months. The long separation had the desired effect and the love affair burned out. Another threat to the dignity of the Crown had been banished.

Standards seemed to have dropped even more alarmingly in 1982 when the Queen's own personal bodyguard, Commander Michael Trestrail, resigned because he had become involved with a money-hungry male prostitute, Michael Rauch. The man who protected the sovereign's life was revealed as a dangerous security risk. His sometime lover Rauch tried to squeeze £15,000 out of the *Sun* newspaper for the story of their seedy affair. The newspaper turned him down and contacted officials at Buckingham Palace who, in turn, informed Scotland Yard. An investigation revealed that Trestrail had been sent blackmail letters and the Queen's chief bodyguard was a ruined man.

As a result of that scandal Royal Protection officers became more closely screened for homosexual connections. Afterwards, several junior officers with gay tendencies quietly left the squad. One of them was in the team which guards the Prince and Princess of Wales.

Gay employees created more domestic dramas within the Palace. A former 'straight' footman once revealed: 'It was impossible not to be aware of the number of homosexuals among the staff. One night a man tried to commit suicide after his gay love affair ended and he chose a room directly above the Queen's bedroom to finish it all. However, he was found just in time and his life saved. The Master of the Household wanted to sack him but the Queen wouldn't hear of it. "No, no, we must help this poor man," she insisted.'

An inquiry aboard the Royal Yacht *Britannia* resulted in two sailors leaving the Royal Navy and two more being suspended.

Closer to the throne and therefore far more damaging were claims that Princess Michael of Kent, wife of the Queen's cousin, was romantically involved with a Texan tycoon. This outlandish lady committed so many other gaffes that almost all her neighbours at Kensington Palace shunned her. She publicly criticised her husband and told him: 'Try not to look stupid' when they posed for pictures together. Despite her rank and privileges she moaned about not receiving a handout from the taxpayers in the Civil List and became an obvious embarrassment to her in-laws. Yet she still remained on the guest list at Windsor Castle each Christmas. When troubles appear the Windsors close ranks to limit the damage to the entire clan.

The twentieth century has presented the Royal Family with many such problems that they have never had to face before. And it is a tribute to the Queen's common sense that she has hung on to the public's high regard despite the crises and disasters her family have become involved in.

But the cumulative effect of all these sensational incidents must be of great concern. Just one really sordid scandal or a major controversy could precipitate the final crisis. And no one can predict what that may be.

When Prince Charles visited Italy in 1985 he fully intended to show his belief in ecumenical ideas by being present at a mass in the Vatican celebrated by Pope John Paul II. But as heir to the throne Prince Charles was forbidden by the 1701 Act of Settlement from marrying a Catholic. If he had done so the monarchy would have been dangerously threatened. To take communion with the Pope would have had dire consequences.

So his mother, fearful that anti-Papist elements in her kingdom would rise up in outrage against this, forced her son to give up his plan. Both the Roman Church and the Prince were embarrassed by the Queen's intervention but she was adamant that her family must stay well away from any religious controversy.

While the Queen herself has remained irreproachable and far above the undignified messes her relatives become involved in, her immediate heirs are another matter.

The monarchy may be more popular than ever according to public opinion polls, but respect for each individual rises and falls constantly. The Prince of Wales has been the subject of a certain amount of ridicule in TV comedy shows as well as in some sections of the press.

His enthusiastic support for a controversial cancer treatment, organic farming methods and other 'alternative' practices have led to the media portraying him as an endearing duffer out of touch with mainstream opinion. His trek into the Kalahari and working holiday on an island in the Hebrides created the idea of the 'Hermit Prince' and questions were raised about his mental health.

Will he get the same lack of respect when he becomes king? And if so will his subjects take him seriously as their Head of State? Every tiny incident is like a drop of water gradually wearing away the foundation stones of the monarchy. A constant trickle can eventually do as much damage as a sudden flood.

The marriage of the Prince and Princess of Wales plays a vital part in maintaining the popularity of the entire Windsor family. The romance between the dashing Prince and his demure bride was a storybook affair that captivated the world.

Then the royal bride went through a difficult period of adjustment. This was not the fairytale ending the public expected. This royal marriage was not supposed to hit the snags which ordinary couples encounter.

Consider for a moment what would happen if they *should* encounter serious problems in the relationship. It may be just a flight of fancy but it should never be totally ruled out. One in three marriages now end in a divorce court and royals seem no better than ordinary folk when it comes to avoiding romantic pitfalls. Could Charles and Diana ever get a divorce?

The general opinion remains that even a legal separation would be impossible. Royal observers believe that even if they seriously fell out the royal couple would soldier on simply for the sake of duty. But if a parting eventually became unavoidable would this be the scandal that would topple the House of Windsor?

No doubt about it, today Charles without Diana seems unthinkable. But the unthinkable keeps happening to the Queen's family. Who would ever have believed that an intruder in Buckingham Palace would reach the inner sanctum of the Queen's own bedroom? It was a fantastically far-fetched thought until it happened.

The Queen's former press secretary Michael Shea, who writes thrillers in his spare time, once said he would never write a book about Charles and Diana. 'I couldn't cope with it novelistically,' he explained. 'It's too strange. You know, truth is stranger than fiction.' Even he believes this couple are exceptional. So a divorce may seem improbable but it is not impossible.

If the Prince and Princess did confound us all, their parting would almost certainly have far-reaching effects on the monarchy. As the future Defender of the Faith how could Prince Charles seek to dissolve a union blessed by the Church of England? Such a scandal would no doubt bring about a major split between Church and State. The result would be a future king left without a consort to share the burden of his lonely position. And when he was crowned king what would become of the mother of his children? Would she be excluded from the Coronation? Or even exiled from the Court?

Diana would certainly lose her title Princess of Wales, as well as her children. As heirs to the throne they belong to the nation rather than to their mother. She would probably be forced to flee from the furore and might take refuge at her mother's sheep station in Australia, where she hid from the world in 1981 shortly before her engagement.

Princess Diana has played an important part in renewing interest in the eccentric old institution of the monarchy. Her youth, charm and sheer glamour have injected new life into a rather stuffy family. Like an Afghan hound among Corgis she stands out among the other royal ladies. Her impact on the Royal House of Windsor has been astounding. Today she is the only member of the family who can make news simply by turning up somewhere. It seems now that they simply cannot do without her.

Diana used to tease pressmen who pursued her: 'Oh, I know you'll all grow tired of me one day when Prince Andrew runs off and marries some exotic beauty.' And, of course, in the end the sailor prince threw all the models and actresses overboard and found safe harbour with a nice, well-bred girl the family approved of. But fun-loving Fergie, the instantly popular Duchess of York, has still not come close to eclipsing Diana – despite her daredevil tricks, looping-the-loop with the Red Devils or making funny faces for cameramen.

Diana's international appeal is far greater than that of any other member of the family. She is regarded as the older generation's ideal daughter while equally popular with the young. She is one of a handful of almost mythical celebrities who are famous in every corner of the earth. For this reason any scandal which involved her would be far more damaging. But despite her unshakeable position as the royal Golden Girl Diana does not seem to have been cast in the same mould as the other powerful women of Windsor.

When the Queen Mother and eventually the Queen die the monarchy may suddenly be left without any firm hand on the tiller. For more than thirty-five years Elizabeth II has steered her family safely through the crises and disasters that have afflicted her reign; she is in firm control of the House of Windsor. But when she is gone will her son, tortured by doubts about his role, become such a steady captain at the helm?

The Queen found herself beset by doubts when as an inexperienced twenty-five-year-old she inherited the throne. She felt lost without the guiding hand of her father and turned for advice to the courtiers King George VI had trusted. At times she was not well served by the old guard at the Palace, as events later proved. But she followed the line laid down by tradition and slowly raised the monarchy to new heights of popularity.

Prince Charles has already proved that he does not always agree with his advisers and several have resigned as a result. Once he is on the throne a split between the King and his courtiers could develop into a constitutional crisis. Which side would the government be on?

It is one of the extraordinary aspects of the monarchy that at a time of great grief the new King will be expected to establish himself firmly on the throne and maintain the continuity of the Crown.

A smoother transition from one reign to the next could be guaranteed if the Queen abdicated in favour of her son. But despite public opinion being in favour of such a step the Queen has no intention of quitting. She is determined to wear the crown until the day she dies. The spectre of her uncle's abdication makes her too nervous to consider anything but a natural break in the line of succession.

A highly placed official at Church House in London explained the legal and religious complications which affect the Queen's decision. 'First the Queen is the Defender of the Faith, the nominal head of the Church of England. At her Coronation in 1953, unlike the Dutch or Swedish monarchs, she was anointed Queen. This is virtually the same as becoming a priest. In the eyes of the Church she can never be un-anointed. She is Queen for life.

'Under the Act of Settlement all the heirs of King George IV reign for life. You would have to have an Act of Parliament to change this. Legally, that would be a simple matter: Parliament can do anything. Of course, it has never happened in the past thousand years. The only monarchs who have walked or been shoved out still alive were not crowned. And then, there is another consideration. Elizabeth II is not just Queen of England but Queen of Australia, Canada, New Zealand and other Commonwealth countries. So they would all have to be consulted too. Many of them might be against the idea of abdication and if the Queen persisted in her wish to step down this could lead to the break-up of the Commonwealth. The Queen would never risk that after she has spent her life preserving it.'

The break-up of the Commonwealth would very probably lead to the end of the monarchy in countries like Australia, where the majority of the people are now of non-British origin. That in turn could lead to the British people asking if they really needed the Windsors too. In a climate of political unrest it would take only a forceful and charismatic left-wing figure to get a republican bandwagon rolling right across the country.

For the first time in centuries the nation might start asking some tricky questions about the privileged characters born to carry on a family profession dating back through forty-two reigns to William the Conqueror.

Are they worthy upholders of the most magical institution on earth? Or are they just glitzy performers in a long-running theatrical production – props of the past no longer needed by a modern society? The role of the monarchy at the beginning of the twenty-first century has yet to be analysed. What do the members of the Royal Family actually do for us?

Some people argue that they are the icing on the British cake. They present a pretty picture to the rest of the world of what life in this ancient kingdom is all about. The pomp and pageantry of royal occasions add a dignity to official life which is generally lacking in republican countries.

The British nation – and other nations – enjoy looking at them; tourists flock to Britain every time a major royal event occurs. Everyone adores the Royal House of Windsor. Their immense prestige right around the globe makes them a national asset.

Anyone who feels that the £5,661,200 the taxpayers fork out annually to keep the Queen's family in business is a waste of money is guilty of short-sightedness. Our top Royals are a super sales team whose overseas tours are also increasingly vital in winning new export orders. The Queen's 1986 visit to China resulted in nineteen new trade agreements being signed.

Two for telecommunications equipment involved an immediate £50 million, and the rest are expected to reap multi-million-pound benefits.

Another great success was the visit by Charles and Diana to the Gulf States the same year. Export orders jumped by 20 per cent even though the Saudi Arabians, hit by falling oil prices, were cutting their imports. Obviously, while they produce such great dividends it makes economic sense to keep the firm of Windsor & Co. in business indefinitely.

But neither the Queen nor her son Charles rely on their sales chart continuing to soar upwards. Always at the back of their minds are words of warning from Lord Louis Mountbatten, the man who was something of an expert on disappearing dynasties. He had seen his Romanoff Russian cousins, the family of Czar Nicholas II, wiped out by revolutionaries in 1918. He had spent childhood holidays with Queen Alexandra of Yugoslavia whose throne was toppled in 1941. His own nephew, the Queen's husband, had become a refugee when the Greek Royal Family was driven into exile.

Once when invited to bet on the chances of the British monarchy surviving through the twenty-first century Lord Louis looked doubtful. He would not gamble on the fortunes of the Windsors beyond the reign of King Charles III, he said. From then on the fate of the Royal Family would depend on whoever inherited the throne next. One royal rotter would mean the doom of the whole dynasty, he warned.

The monarchy could only ever be as good as the people doing the job, he explained. 'If we produce a royal failure,' he used to say, 'we shall not be let off the hook again.'

12

King and Consort

On Christmas Day some years ago a servant at Windsor Castle looked out of a window just as the wintry afternoon light was beginning to fade. In the courtyard below outside St George's Chapel he saw three figures busily picking up litter left by crowds who had earlier gathered to watch the Royal Family attend the Christmas Day service.

Like millions of other people in Britain who had just enjoyed an enormous Christmas dinner, Prince Andrew and Prince Edward had been slumped in front of the TV watching the Queen's speech when Prince Charles found them. As soon as their mother's image faded from the screen he had dragged his brothers out of the warm drawing room and put them to work in the cold.

Realising that the Castle staff, who normally keep the grounds immaculate, were also taking a day off, the Prince had decided to do the job himself. And he had roped in Andrew and Edward to help before dusk closed in.

As the amazed Castle employee watched, Charles kept urging a rather reluctant Andrew and Edward to help him clean up the paths and lawn. And he wasn't satisfied until every crisp packet, every empty soft drink can and chocolate wrapper had been shoved into a large plastic sack.

It was a thoughtful gesture, typical of the caring Prince, to save someone else extra work over the holidays. It was also a clue to the character of the man who will one day be a king,

167

yet is touchingly desperate to be ordinary. He constantly tries to prove, perhaps more to himself than anyone else, that despite the titles and wealth which place him far above ordinary men, he is still on their level.

He often washes down his own ponies after he plays polo and confides to his friends that he believes the Royal Family have too many inherited privileges. He loves what he calls 'roughing it' at Craigowan, his lodge on the Balmoral estate, where he often spends a week without his valet or chauffeur. He polishes his own shoes and drives off to fill his car up with petrol delighted to be doing what 'normal' people do.

His constant search to find a way to make his privileged life meaningful is not likely to end when he comes to the throne. His reign will be dedicated to bringing the people in the Palace closer to those who live outside.

He has always looked for ways to bridge this gap. On a skiing holiday in Klosters with Lady Sarah Spencer some years ago he was offered VIP treatment. To avoid queues of skiers waiting to catch the lifts to the mountain top he was led through a special door by German police and permitted to have sole use of the next car that arrived.

The following morning he refused offers of the same special service and insisted on joining the long line of people waiting at the ski-lift. About twenty minutes passed before he reached the head of the queue, and just as he did the waiting car filled up and the doors closed. Shaking his head as he was forced to stand back Charles commented: 'This is a very democratic country.'

One man on his staff once summed up the Prince's appealing lack of snobbery. 'He never reminds you who he is until you forget.' But despite his efforts to remain humble and selfless, his ingrained pride occasionally gets the better of him. This happened once when the Prince joined the Queen Mother to have lunch with her lady-in-waiting, Ruth, Lady Fermoy, who is Princess Diana's grandmother. They were staying at Sandringham and set off in plenty of time to reach the hotel where the Queen Mother's best friend was waiting.

The chauffeur, Arthur Bartlett, was not familiar with the district and Prince Charles had to confess he didn't know which road to take either. Eventually the driver decided to stop and ask an old man by the roadside for directions.

He soon got the right information from the elderly gentleman who did not bother to glance at the passengers in the back of the Range Rover even once. As they set off again Prince Charles looked back in amazement at the man and said: 'I don't think he realised who we were. Fancy that!' Charles is thrilled when he can go out anywhere without being spotted, unaware that country folk on royal estates often turn a blind eye to his presence out of respect for his privacy.

But royal employees who have known the Prince for many years believe that his love of being ordinary reveals a Walter Mitty-like character who refuses to face living in one world and tries constantly to escape into another.

'All this milking cows on the Duchy of Cornwall farms and planting potatoes in the Hebrides is a sign of his restlessness with his royal position,' claims one man who has known the Prince most of his life. 'I think he is very confused. He doesn't seem to know what sort of life he really wants. And I suspect that he is not tough enough to be a good king. He is much too indecisive.'

The Prince is always worried that people don't take him seriously and therefore he cannot make any great contribution. He is forever telling the organisers of charities he is involved with: 'I don't want to be just a name on the letterhead, you know. I want to be really involved and be of some use.'

He has always been anxious to find ways to prove his worthiness to the British people. He felt frustrated and angry when his younger brother Andrew was allowed to put his life on the line for his country during the Falklands conflict while he was forced to watch from the sidelines. He would have liked to win his spurs in battle, and prove himself like his ancestor the Black Prince who led his people to victory in the fourteenth century. Security advisers put an end to that dream.

Now Charles hopes to lead a moral crusade that will make

Britain a better place for everyone to live in. He is determined to be more than just a caring king. He wants to initiate an era of change. When he rules in his mother's place, many Palace workers believe, he will abolish many of the pastimes the Queen indulges in. The annual royal house party at Windsor during Ascot week in June is unlikely to be carried on into the next reign, they claim.

While preserving respect for the throne he is anxious to abolish meaningless tributes to members of the royal family. By the end of the century curtseys and other forms of bowing and scraping seem certain to become as obsolete as sending royal enemies to the Tower. And more members of his family may be earning their own living.

Friends like Sir Laurens van der Post hope he will go down in history as Charles the Reformer, a man determined to become a great influence for good on the monarchy. They believe he will become an inspiration and an example to the world of what his motto, 'I Serve', really means.

The Prince, while admiring his mother's achievements, has plans to do things differently. The problems of disadvantaged young people, and disillusioned minorities are his particular concern. Solving the unemployment problem, he believes, will cure a lot of other social ills, and he has concentrated on finding ways to alleviate it. He has gained a tremendous feeling of satisfaction from his work with Business in the Community; by badgering big businesses to lend their expertise to people who want to start up their own companies he has achieved more than any other member of his family. He has actually helped to improve opportunities for ordinary people and he is spurred on in this work by his private fears of one day ruling a divided nation

Another top priority is his plan to introduce more people from different backgrounds into Buckingham Palace, though at present he does not have the authority to overrule the Queen's advisers who claim his ideas smack of 'positive discrimination'. He had been hoping to recruit some staff from non-white Commonwealth countries on to his household. For several years he has employed a soldier from the Gurkhas as an odd-job man at Kensington Palace, but he also wanted to employ some office workers of different racial backgrounds.

In May 1983 a West Indian secretary left Buckingham Palace because she felt uncomfortable among the exclusively Sloane Ranger office staff. Prince Charles was very disappointed when she resigned and ever since he has been trying to encourage his aides to hire staff more representative of the population at large.

He has also made an effort to increase the number of black faces among the top Army regiments of the Household Division. And he has made it clear that by the time he becomes king he expects to see more coloured officers on duty at ceremonies like Trooping the Colour. But Army top brass have repeatedly protested to the Prince that they recruit and promote people on the grounds of merit alone. Already he is choosing friends and advisers from many different backgrounds, unlike his mother who throughout her reign has stuck to the same group of wealthy aristocrats.

He also feels that more handicapped people should be given jobs on the Queen's staff, and is determined to be an equal opportunities employer when he takes over. He explains that installing ramps for wheelchairs alongside the stairs between different levels of the ground floor in Buckingham Palace would be no problem, and most office doorways in this elegant mansion are already wide enough.

The fiercest opposition to his plans is believed to have come from his father. The Duke of Edinburgh feels his son has good intentions but is not aware of the complications involved in his idealistic schemes. He wonders how handicapped people who applied for jobs but were rejected would feel and thinks the result could be more bad feeling than good.

The Iron Duke is so opposed to many of his son's plans that father and son are no longer close. At one point their disagreements became so bitter that the two men made a point of avoiding each other. Philip was especially irritated when Charles, full of the joys of new fatherhood, decided to undertake fewer public engagements after the birth of Prince

Harry. Annoyed that his son was devoting more time to his family than his duty, the Duke did not bother to visit his new grandchild.

Aware that the Queen was deeply concerned about the situation, Prince Charles has made a great effort to heal the rift. He took up shooting again so he could spend more time in the Duke's company. When he gave up the sport several years ago many people believed it was the result of pleas from his soft-hearted wife not to shoot game. But Diana was raised a country girl and has no qualms about picking up bloody, freshly killed partridge or pheasant after a shoot. The real reason the Prince put down his Purdy shotguns was that he had become bored.

The estate manager at Sandringham, where the Royal Family shoot most often, always gave the Prince the best position in the middle of the stand. Although he is one of the best shots in the country, he could hardly fail to miss when so many birds were driven by the beaters straight towards him. He grew tired of potting helpless, terrified birds because it was simply too easy.

Now he is shooting again but insists on being on the outside of the stand where fewer birds fly over and more skill is required to bring them down. Prince William often arrives with the Queen to have lunch with the guns. If he behaves throughout the meal he is allowed afterwards to stand behind his father wearing his own pair of earmuff protectors. The small Prince watches proudly as his father cleanly drops dozens of birds, and when the gundogs bring them in William helps to pile them into the game bags.

But taking up once again the field sport which his father loves so much has not done much to bring Charles and the Duke closer. One man who has regularly joined Sandringham shoots says: 'The Prince always tells his father he would love to join in and then he is the last to arrive. The Duke gets furious waiting for him because winter days are short and they are wasting good daylight hanging about wondering when the Prince of Wales will turn up. Some days when he is very late the Duke doesn't speak to him for the rest of the entire day. It is very awkward for everyone else when this happens. The Duke is often grumpy enough, anyway, because the recoil when he shoots inflames the arthritis in his shoulders. We don't need Prince Charles making his bad temper worse.'

Estate workers have also seen both men set off for long walks around the Norfolk fields and hedgerows, but they always go separately. The royal rift appears to be unbridgeable.

It is a sign of Charles' complex character that although he doesn't mind keeping his father waiting, knowing that it infuriates him, he hates being kept hanging about himself.

When he arrived at Matsapha airport at the end of a visit to Swaziland in March 1987 the Prince was told that the country's teenage King Mswati III had suddenly decided to drive out to say an unscheduled goodbye.

Although they had earlier said farewell the world's youngest king was anxious to make his British visitor feel he had been very welcome. But Prince Charles soon discovered that he had become a victim of a happy disregard for timekeeping. The time for departure came and went and still there was no sign of King Mswati. Charles paced up and down on the tarmac looking at his watch and asking British Embassy officials: 'What's the delay?' They could only shrug their shoulders and use the old Africa hand's expression AWA. As one man who has served below the Equator for many years told him: 'It means Africa wins again. Whenever anything goes wrong that would never happen back home we say it's another case of AWA.'

This was not much consolation to Prince Charles who was getting worried that his four-hour flight to Malawi would be held up so long that he would be late for his official arrival there. His Royal Air Force VC10 was ready for take-off but the Prince was forced to wait twenty minutes before the young king cruised up in his Lincoln Continental apparently unaware that he had created a problem.

Group Captain Marcus Wills who is in charge of the Queen's Flight later explained why Prince Charles had been so edgy.

'The Royal Air Force prides itself on being punctual. By leaving Swaziland late we looked certain to be behind schedule arriving in Malawi where we knew President Banda was waiting with an official guard of honour to welcome the Prince of Wales. We did not have enough time on the short flight to make up the lost time.

'So the Prince had a terrible choice to make. He could either leave on time and risk offending the King of Swaziland, or touch down in Blantyre, Malawi, late and keep a President waiting. In the end, we sent a message ahead to inform the officials at the airport in Blantyre that we would be delayed.'

A month later on a tour of Spain Prince Charles was delayed again. As he piloted his aircraft into Barajas airport Spanish air traffic controllers kept him stacked up over Madrid and made him take his turn before landing. When he was finally given clearance to descend he was directed to the wrong end of the airport and was ten minutes behind schedule when he taxied to a halt on the tarmac.

Later that day he explained: 'Do you know what? Those Spanish air traffic controllers thought I was a cargo plane. They sent us to a cargo bay. I kept following their directions when I landed, thinking it was a very peculiar place for an official arrival but I couldn't argue. Then they redirected me to the right place. That's why we were so late.'

Another contradiction in his character is his well-known stinginess. All his clothes are sent to a south London laundry, but the cost-conscious Prince makes his valets wash his dirty handkerchiefs. When he sent them out with the rest of his washing they often went missing in transit. No one knew how or where they vanished but the Prince suspected people used to take them as souvenirs because they bore the Prince of Wales three-feathered emblem.

He was appalled by the high cost of furnishing Highgrove and grumpily paid the bills after endless checks of all the items. He always moans about the ever-rising housekeeping budget and has been known to inspect the fridge to see if staff are ordering too much food. He goes around his London home switching lights off to save pence and gets annoyed if he finds a television set left blaring with no one watching it. And yet he keeps his ancient Aston Martin sports car, which his mother gave him for his twenty-first birthday, although he drives it only five months of the year. And the fact that it gobbles up petrol at an alarming rate doesn't bother him.

His staff say that he is not a mean-spirited man. In fact, he is quite the opposite, the kindest, most understanding person most of them have ever met. So why is he so mean with money? 'It's my Scottish blood,' Charles explains with a grin. 'I just can't help it.' This is not quite true because whenever he stays at the homes of friends he leaves generous tips for their staff and also puts a large cash donation on the plate when he goes to church.

Some people close to Charles reckon he has a begging bowl mentality. They say his tight-fisted behaviour is the result of being riddled with guilt about the comfortable life he leads when he sees such deprivation everywhere he goes. He knows that only an accident of birth is responsible for his privileged position and feels he has to justify it endlessly. They point out he is not a grudging giver and devotes a huge amount of his time to charitable works. He is only miserly with himself, as if feeling he has to experience going without to experience what life is like for ordinary people.

The next king is a man who is buffeted about by many conflicting influences. He stopped eating red meat when a polo-playing friend told him he would get fitter eating only white meat. Now he has dropped the idea. He was once keen on playing the cello but stopped playing it when he realised he would never become a skilled musician because he did not have enough time to practise.

At present he is passionate about gardening. He loves it so much he even devotes hours to producing bumper crops of organically grown vegetables. Then he packages them up and sends Highgrove carrots and beans to friends as gifts. But his wife, aware that his passions wax and wane regularly, says: 'Oh I know he loves his garden, but as soon as he has finished sorting out every inch of it he will get bored with it and take up something else. He's like that.'

In many ways the differences between Charles and Diana make them perfectly complement each other. His dreamy approach to life is balanced by her down-to-earth attitude. Diana is very much a woman of her times whereas Charles, for all his popularity, is out of step with his own generation.

In his genteel, other-worldly way he is shocked if anyone makes a risqué joke in front of a woman. When he asked me once if I knew another reporter standing nearby I said I did. The journalist he referred to was a quip-witted character, who immediately chipped in with a joke: 'Oh yes, we have known each other for years but not in the biblical sense, of course.' The Prince laughed feebly with a look of alarm that anyone should make such an indelicate remark in front of a lady.

His wife, on the other hand, is much more likely to shock than be shocked herself. While chatting to journalists once about bygone days before her marriage, when she was being pursued by the press, Diana said she remembered everything vividly. 'Do you remember how I was then?' she asked coquettishly. 'I used to have lots up top, remember? Well it's all gone now, isn't it,' she sighed. And with both hands clasped across her chest she showed them just what she meant. The two men she was talking to were Harry Arnold and his colleague photographer Arthur Edwards. In their long careers following the Royal Family they had heard some amazing stories. But they had never imagined that one day the future Queen of England would be discussing the size of her boobs with them. They gulped and looked at each other amazed. For once this chatty pair were lost for words.

If Prince Charles sincerely wishes to be as 'ordinary' as he claims, he should take lessons from his wife. Her common touch has opened a lot of windows in the Palace and set a wind of change blowing many cobwebby old ideas away. Diana talks to the people she meets on their own level. She always has done. 'Would you like to see my ring?' she asked guests at a Buckingham Palace garden party soon after her engagement. Then she added beaming: 'I have to be careful, I keep scratching my nose with my ring. It's so big – the ring, that is, not my nose!'

Her jokes, teasing and confessions about her own faults make nervous people she meets feel relaxed in her company. Her interests are the same as the ordinary people she meets. When she met Anna Carteret, the star of the BBC TV drama series about a policewoman, Juliet Bravo, Diana asked: 'Did you know I dressed up as a police officer too?' The actress replied that she had indeed read reports in the newspapers about the Princess and her friend Fergie posing as police constables to fool Prince Andrew. 'Of course, I didn't look as good as you did,' Diana added flatteringly.

When she goes away on tour Diana leaves instructions for staff to video all her favourite soap operas. She particularly likes to keep up with the doings of Dirty Den and the other EastEnders stars. And she still pops out to visit her favourite supermarket, Sainsburys in the Cromwell Road, west London, wearing a scarf over her head to avoid recognition. She hunts for health foods to give her sons but when they come home from school, she says, they turn their little noses up at her treats. 'I'm afraid they'd rather eat the things that are bad for them just like all children,' she admits. Her instantaneous rapport with people from all walks of life is a natural gift – and a tremendous asset for a future queen.

But there is some evidence that although the public think that when they come to the throne, King Charles and his consort Diana will be a sensational team, some members of their own family are not so sure.

Prince Philip, concerned that his son is too soft and indecisive to tackle some of the tougher aspects of the job, also wonders if Diana's superstar image has trivialised the monarchy. Princess Anne also loses patience with her brother's soul-searching and has never got along very well with his wife. She showed what she thought of her scene-stealing sister-in-law when she snubbed Diana and Charles by failing to turn up at the christening of their second baby, Prince Harry. While every other Royal was at Windsor witnessing the baptism and then wetting the baby's head with champagne afterwards, Anne went out shooting pheasants instead.

Only days later when the two women were brought together to celebrate Christmas with the Queen, Anne ruined the season of goodwill by having furious row with Charles about his wife. She called her brother a 'wimp' for taking orders from Diana and yelled: 'I will not be pushed around by that brainless woman.'

Despite the frosty atmosphere that persists between the two, Diana devotes a lot of time to Anne's children, Peter and Zara. As their mother often works right through their school holidays Diana makes sure they have a good time when they visit royal estates with the Queen.

Staff at Sandringham have noticed that when Diana and Charles take William out on a sledge in the snow during their winter break, they always invite Anne's children along. 'Their squeals of laughter can be heard all over the grounds,' explains one woman who works at the Big House. 'Charles and Diana haul the children along then take turns swinging them in the air and helping them to organise snowball fights. It is obvious that when she becomes Queen Diana will be the centre of all the love and laughter in the Royal Family. All the younger Royals absolutely adore her.'

The family have always been dominated by strong, positive women from Queen Victoria's time onwards. Prince Charles' great-grandmother Queen Mary, who died in 1953 when he was five, was a living link with Victorian times. She believed all her family should make any sacrifice in the name of duty. When her eldest son David refused to listen to her pleas and gave up the throne it broke her heart. But she kept her hold on the reins of power through her second son, Bertie, when he became King George VI.

Her daughter-in-law Elizabeth, the Queen Mother, replaced her as the family matriarch and now she is the person everyone turns to for advice. In particular, she has often been more of a mother to her grandson Charles than her daughter had time to be. She nursed him through bouts of homesickness when he went to Gordonstoun School and later listened when he poured out tales of unhappy love affairs. She summed up her grandson once better perhaps than any other member of his family has ever done when she described him as 'a boy with a very gentle heart'.

In spite of her famous charm Diana is not chummy enough with her husband's relatives to replace the Queen Mother as the next royal matriarch. That is a role more likely to be taken by her best friend Fergie: the Duchess of York has the special knack of being liked by women and of being pally with men. Although attractive, she certainly never looks like stealing Diana's crown as Queen of Style, but as her own family eventually grow up around her Fergie will be the link that holds the family together.

Prince Charles has always been fond of her, Diana confides in her, and Princess Anne shares her love of the horses, hounds and headscarf set. Fergie can even sweet talk the Duke of Edinburgh into a good mood. She is his chief helper when he organises family barbecues and gets everyone in a good mood. The dedicated Duchess is the superglue sort that binds broken relationships and restores a smooth finish.

Fergie entered the royal ranks when she was twenty-six. By then she clearly knew what she was letting herself in for. The Princess of Wales had been her close friend for four years. Diana, by comparison, was an inexperienced teenager when she took on her job.

The girl who nervously walked down the isle of St Paul's to wed her Prince now seems like another person. The chubby-cheeked blonde with the chunky hairdo vanished somewhere between the kindergarten she used to work in and Kensington Palace. A more stylish, more confident woman stands by the side of Prince Charles today. It says a lot for her steely determination that she has come through a period of awesome adjustment and emerged more dazzling than ever.

The coronation of King Charles and his Queen Diana will be the only royal event likely to outshine their wedding celebrations. It will set the seal on a marriage that has fascinated millions ever since it was first announced.

Diana is the Royal Family's insurance policy: Life Before Diana seems bleak in retrospect. Before she arrived the only young women on the royal roadshow were Anne, then known as Princess Sourpuss, and Princess Michael, who was foreign and too far down the pecking order to fill the role of leading lady. Diana stepped into this yawning gap in the royal ranks and a megastar was born.

The family have always been extraordinarily lucky with the consorts they have chosen. Victoria had her Albert, and they became an upper-class Derby and Joan. George VI, the man who never expected to be king, was transformed into one by his devoted Elizabeth, and as the Queen Mother she is still adored by everyone today. Her daughter, the second Elizabeth, married a dashing prince with movie star looks. And now their son has got himself a winner of a wife.

Although Charles definitely calls the shots in his own home, to the world outside he certainly appears to be overshadowed by his glamorous Princess. Her devastating attractiveness has begun to get in the way of their happy marriage. The very quality that makes her such a hit with the masses is affecting their private life together.

Diana is still young at twenty-six and grows more self-assured and stunning with every year that passes. Her husband, meanwhile, is losing his hair and his patience with his soul-destroying job. The only person who can sort out this problem is Diana herself, and already she appears to be very aware that she must take a back seat more often and play down her amazing popularity with the crowds.

When they go out working together now she trails along behind him like a dutiful consort, forever three steps back in her rightful place. Her newly acquired reticence was particularly noticeable during the royal couple's tour of Spain in April 1987. It showed up again when they made a flying twelve-hour visit to the Cannes Film Festival the following month. 'The Princess was dragging along so far back most of the time that the two hardly looked as if they were together,' said one French official.

When they were led into a banquet in honour of the distinguished British actor Sir Alec Guinness their hosts escorted them both around all the dinner tables to show off their prize exhibits. At one point Prince Charles, wondering where the hell they were heading, said sarcastically: 'I think we must be lost.' He wanted the organisers to know that he bitterly resented being paraded around like a prize bull. His wife, thrilled to be in a room with wall-to-wall celebrities, smiled bewitchingly and loved every minute. She knew she belonged. To Charles it was an alien environment and he couldn't wait to escape.

Diana revels in this sort of excitement which her job brings. She adores meeting the world's most glittering personalities, and even more she adores upstaging them all. When she was a small girl she dreamed of becoming a star ballerina but her hopes were dashed when she grew too tall. Now she has found another even better way to hold centre stage. At Cannes she outshone every dazzling star in town and she has never had an acting lesson in her life, she is simply a natural. Diana, the once frustrated performer, has more fame and adoration than she ever dreamed of. Better still, her career as queen will outlast most actresses' popularity.

Looking at her now you get the feeling she could achieve anything. If a baby princess is just what is needed to become the nation's darling and put royal imp Prince William in his place, Diana will no doubt produce a daughter to order. To date she has always got exactly what she wanted out of life and no doubt she always will.

If the Foreign Office wants some churlish head of state from overseas to toe the British line, let Diana work her magic on him. It never fails. British diplomats still joke about the way Diana went to work on Australia's republican-leaning premier Bob Hawke. After the Princess batted those lovely blue eyes at him, all that talk about kicking out the monarchy went very quiet.

In her seven-year hitch the Princess has learned more than

just how to stop her skirts blowing up on a windy day and giving the photographers a leggy shot. She has realised that she is a super saleswoman and the product she is selling is herself. Her success can be seen in the Firm's packed order books. The world can't get enough of its favourite Princess.

On the day she became engaged Diana said she knew she would be OK because she had the help of the man she loved. 'With Charles beside me, I can't go wrong,' she told us. Today, her husband could say exactly the same of Diana with even more feeling.

Bibliography

Charles in His Own Words, compiled by Rosemary York, Omnibus Press, 1981

A Week in the Life of the Royal Family, Weidenfeld & Nicolson, 1983

The Royal Handbook, Alan Hamilton, Mitchell Beazley, 1985

Royal Service, Stephen P. Barry, Angus & Robertson (Australia), 1983

The Reality of the Monarchy, Andrew Duncan, William Heinemann Ltd, 1970

Atlas of Royal Britain, Windward, 1984

Prince Charles Horseman, Michael Clayton, Stanley Paul, 1987

Diana Princess of Wales, The Book of Fashion, Jane Owen, Colour Library Books, 1983

In Private, In Public, the Prince and Princess of Wales, Alastair Burnet, Michael O'Mara, 1986

Royal Children, Nicholas Courtney, J. M. Dent & Co., 1982

Charles Prince of Wales, Anthony Holden, Weidenfeld & Nicolson, 1979